WALK IN MY SHOES

WALK IN MY SHOES

An Anthology on Usher Syndrome

Edited by Charlotte J. DeWitt

Merrimack Media

Boston, Massachusetts

CONTENTS

In Praise of Walk in My Shoes   xi

Foreword   1

PART I. DIAGNOSIS: LEARNING, ACCEPTING, LIVING WITH USHER SYNDROME

1. THROUGH LILLY'S EYES: A MOTHER'S INTERPRETATION   5
A young mother tells of her daughter Lilly's Usher diagnosis and their journey to raise awareness and raise funds for research.
Angela Diuble

2. MY JOURNEY TO AN USHER DIAGNOSIS   13
A delayed diagnosis propelled this author into political activism so others would not have to wait for help.
Laura Rough

3. MY LITTLE SECRET   19
The challenge... and stress... of hiding Usher from family and friends. Early onset blindness at age 22.
Randi Knutson

4. LIFE WITH A LATE USHER DIAGNOSIS   29
A native of Madrid, Spain, this author's Usher condition went undetected for years because she was so good at coping. Educated in the UK and the US, she continues to inspire with her many achievements.
Marisa Herrera Postlewate, PhD

PART II. LIFE IN AN USHER FAMILY

5. FEARING THE UNKNOWN 41
A mother talks about the difficulties adopting a
child as an Usher parent, raising two children, and
learning to live life to its fullest.
Anna Sengillo

6. LIFE WITH A MOM WHO HAS USHER 51
SYNDROME
Anna Sengillo's two children share their stories,
both humorous and compassionate, about life with
their Usher mother.
Jesse & Candice Sengillo

7. MY LIFE ADJUSTMENTS WITH USHER 57
From a diagnosis of deafness at age 2 to impending
blindness as a single mother with both Usher
syndrome and Coats disease at 23, Jenni trains for a
new career and refuses to give up. This is a story
with a very happy ending.
Jenni Thompson

8. A CHILD'S POINT OF VIEW 63
As her mother loses more sight and hearing, Jenni
Thompson's 15-year-old daughter finds inspiration
and a role model on being strong … even though
she, too, could have a child with Usher syndrome in
later life.
Cheyenne Thompson

9. SCALING MOUNTAINS 67
The mother of two USH1F girls talks about
exploring communication alternatives… and
making history.
Melissa Chaikof

10. SEARCHING FOR THE LIGHT IN THE 83
DARKNESS
The youngest person ever to receive a cochlear
implant writes of her challenges from Girl Scout
camp to college chemistry classes.
Jessica Chaikof

11. IT'S ALWAYS CHRISTMAS   89
    With great humor and insight, a mother shares her
    interior decorating tips adapting her home to make
    daily life easier for her adult Usher 1 son.
    Karen Duke

PART III. INDEPENDENT LIVING

12. THE BLINDING DRIVE AND BEYOND   99
    A young woman driving a Camaro sports car at
    night suddenly cannot see and must come to terms
    with coping with Usher... or else.
    Sonya Marney

13. BEING INDEPENDENT WITH USHER   111
    "I come from a family where all women are
    warriors, and I intend to do the same," writes the
    author, a native of Mexico. Bilingual in English and
    Spanish, she shares her tips on how to adapt as an
    international IT professional, and how to succeed
    in living a fulfilling life in spite of Usher and
    retinitis pigmentosa.
    Diana Velarde

14. TRANSITIONING WITH USHER   123
    SYNDROME
    "Would you rather be blind or deaf?" was a survey
    question in junior high school. Years later, with the
    help of a leader dog, the author makes the
    transition from living sighted to being deafblind.
    Sharon James

15. THE POWER OF THE CANE   133
    Who says cane training can't be funny? Some of the
    most unique ideas ever on what to do with a white
    cane.
    Randall DeWitt

16. TEN THOUSAND MILES FROM HOME 143
   A congenitally blind student graduates and chooses
   to relocate so as to teach geographically isolated
   Usher 1 people orientation and mobility skills.
   Lelan Miller

17. INDEPENDENCE DAY 153
   Ever curious, the aunt of an Usher 1 man tries her
   hand as a deafblind person with a white cane on the
   4th of July to show the obstacles and often
   impossible accessibility issues present in the city of
   Boston. The hurricane was extra.
   Charlotte J. DeWitt

PART IV. PROFESSIONAL LIFE AS AN USHER
PERSON

18. WHEN ONE DOOR CLOSES 161
   A teacher of English as a Second Language
   repatriates after an overseas posting and re-invents
   herself as an exhibitor in arts and crafts shows in
   America.
   Amy Bovaird

19. MY USHER'S LIFE LESSONS 169
   A successful attorney adapts, with humor, to a new
   life.
   Mary Dignan

20. REDEFINING INDEPENDENCE AND 177
   EMPOWERMENT
   The author reflects on the 9,280 days since she was
   first diagnosed with Usher syndrome, her career as
   a school psychologist, and the pivotal moment of
   giving up her driver's license.
   Roberta Giordano

21. AN ODYSSEY THROUGH USHER 189
   An IT professional moves overseas and shows how
   access to transportation is the key to professional
   advancement.
   Mani Iyer

22. STEPPING STONES   201

After intensive mobility training wearing blinders
to learn self-confidence using a white cane, a brave
young woman moves to China to teach in an
orphanage.
Audrey Chard

PART V. INSPIRING TALES: WHO SAYS I
CAN'T?

23. RACING AGAINST TIME   211

A bank manager tackles the onset of deafness and
blindness by defiantly founding a social club for
Usher women, producing conferences for the blind,
influencing politics at the state level, and initiating
this book project—all while dealing cheerfully and
positively with major health issues of her own. "No"
is not in her vocabulary, and she never quits.
Ramona Rice

24. HOW TO GET A MINOR IN A FOREIGN   217
LANGUAGE WHEN YOU HAVE USHER

A young college student gets lost in Germany and
survives using his new language skills powered by
an invincible, can-do attitude.
Brian Switzer

25. TETHERED IN STRIDES   223

An artist, photographer, copywriter, and marathon
runner, this spunky author's motto is "My horizon
is broader than my tunnel vision." She urges all to
"Walk in My Shoes."
Rose Sarkany

26. MY SELF-DISCOVERY OF USHER   231
    SYNDROME
    Orphaned at birth, now totally deafblind, the
    founder of Seabeck, the annual deafblind
    recreational camp in Seattle, Washington state,
    discusses the challenges of coping with life
    difficulties imposed by the reduction and/or loss of
    five essential values.
    Stephen Ehrlich

27. MY DEAFBLIND LIFE   243
    The founder of the Deaf Blind Community Action
    Network (DBCAN) in Boston and the Deaf Blind
    Association of Connecticut has never let her lack of
    sight or hearing keep her down. She communicates
    primarily via tactile signing and the infectious
    warmth of her personality.
    Elaine Ducharme

    Acknowledgments   249
    Appendix A: An Overview of Usher Syndrome   251
    Appendix B: Resources   254

IN PRAISE OF WALK IN MY SHOES

"*Walk in My Shoes* is a compilation of personal reflections about becoming deafblind. The feeling of courage and dignity is wonderful and will inspire many people—both those who are personally confronting this disability, as well as those who provide support. It is a book about hope and possibility. Congratulations to the many authors for sharing their remarkable stories."
—Marianne Riggio, Director, Educational Leadership Program, Perkins International, Watertown, MA, USA

"*Walk in My Shoes* is an important new publication. The book includes 27 personal stories of individuals moving forward after a diagnosis of Usher syndrome. In reading these stories, one can find a strand of commonality across each writer's experience but also enjoy the diversity of life choices and accomplishments realized. I believe that the book will provide information, support and encouragement to others diagnosed with Usher syndrome, their families, friends, and service providers. Congratulations to the authors and the organizers who brought this project to fruition!"
—Steve Perreault, Helen Keller National Center for Deaf-Blind Youth and Adults, Sands Point, New York, USA

"*Walk in My Shoes* will challenge you to think differently about everything you always thought you knew. As they narrate beautifully written, riveting and often funny stories about such experiences as living overseas as a deafblind person, creating a family and traveling across the U.S. as a software engineer, or establishing a non-profit for people who are visually and hearing impaired, these writers compel readers to bear witness – not to who *they* are, but rather to the potential in all of us. In a spirit of immense generosity 27 writers tell their stories so we can all better understand that in the midst of great difficulty and seemingly impossible obstacles, grit and substance and smarts will prevail. I thank this book's writers and editors, and I promise: I will take up your challenge."

—Megan Sullivan, Associate Dean and Associate Professor at Boston University, Massachusetts, USA, and wife of a deafblind man who has Usher syndrome type 2.

"If you have good vision and hearing, as I do, and even if you have spent most of your career studying the vision of people who are slowly going blind, as I have, you may have some understanding of the process of grieving and adapting that is repeated over and over again as another favorite activity becomes impossible, or another assistive device or program becomes a daily companion. You may, but you still can't fully understand. If this happens to you as a young person in the middle of your education, professional development, and other major life choices, you may lose faith in your ability to survive, let alone thrive.

Imagine, then, that this happens to you while your hearing has been bad from birth or is fading along with your sight. Even if the education system and the Americans with Disabilities Act provide some solutions for the deaf-blind – a term that may not sound politically correct, but let's face it, that's what Usher syndrome is – they can't do the work for you. Not only do you have to overcome countless obstacles to build a life that fulfills your aspirations, you have to convince everyone around you that you won't be defined by your disabilities.

This book is full of inspiring stories, written by some of the most resilient and creative people I have ever met – or hope to meet soon. I feel fortunate to know some of them and call them my friends. I've never walked in their shoes, but these stories have helped me understand what it might be like. I'm glad you'll get to walk alongside them, too, and gain insight into their struggles and triumphs as they continue to discover their potential."

—Gislin Dagnelie, Ph.D., Associate Professor of Ophthalmology, Johns Hopkins University School of Medicine, Baltimore, Maryland, USA

"*Walk in My Shoes* gives a unique and personal insight in to the world of those living with Usher syndrome. Each of the authors tells a powerful story that will pull the reader in to a world of muffled sound and a forever shrinking tunnel of vision. For someone like myself, a person going blind with *retinitis pigmentosa* (RP), the message of the constant battle for independence, the fear of fading loved ones' faces, coupled with dealing with the misconceptions of living with an invisible disability is all too familiar. This collection is a MUST read for anyone affected by sensory loss or those who just want to know more about our world."

—Dave Steele, Poet and author of *Stand By Me RP,* UK

"This is a wonderful book written by wonderful people who are affected by Usher syndrome. Although they have very different paths in life, the one thing that they share is they ensure that life goes on, no matter what the challenges they face whilst living with hearing and sight loss. They overcome those challenges with a steely determination. Whilst adapting to a life with little or no vision or sound, they have the strength to adapt to a different way of doing things, of communicating and above all, a different way of living in a way that ensures a good quality of life. Usher syndrome is not the end. It is the beginning of a new way of living life and overcoming the challenges. A must read for everyone, regardless of ability or disability."

—Carol Brill, Dublin, Ireland, Advocate for Usher syndrome and deafblindness, including a government ministerial appointment; Motivational Speaker; avid golfer with Irish Blind Golf Society.

FOREWORD

Walk in My Shoes takes you to places unseen, unheard, in the most familiar of places—a collection of stories that fill many shoes: diversity, culture, and acceptance.

Imagine walking into a room, seeing the pencil on the floor, and passing by the trumpeting elephant; whispering sweet nothings to a mannequin; or kicking the dreaded yellow "Wet Floor" sign, truly living life like no other. Imagine wearing our shoes every day.

We are all masters of disguise as we trek through the winding paths of emotions and experiences. Tighten up your laces—you are about to walk in our shoes. These are extraordinary chronicles of the not so ordinary.

PART 1

DIAGNOSIS:
LEARNING,
ACCEPTING, LIVING
WITH USHER
SYNDROME

CHAPTER 1

THROUGH LILLY'S EYES: A MOTHER'S INTERPRETATION

A YOUNG MOTHER TELLS OF HER DAUGHTER LILLY'S USHER DIAGNOSIS AND THEIR JOURNEY TO RAISE AWARENESS AND RAISE FUNDS FOR RESEARCH.

ANGELA DIUBLE

L illy Diuble was born three weeks early on a beautiful August day. She was actually due on September 11, 2002. I believe there's something special about summer babies. Lilly just couldn't wait to get the party started, and I believe she did not want to be associated with what had become a somber date for all Americans.

Lilly was my first child. My life blossomed in a way I could not imagine once Lilly entered it. I thought she was perfect! And then, the doctors told me she wasn't.

Lilly was born hearing impaired. I didn't believe it at first, but over time, it turned out to be true. After finally feeling comfortable with juggling a baby with hearing aids, getting her through the toddler stage without losing said hearing aids or ingesting the nickel cadmium batteries inside them, we were finally on a roll.

She was doing great! Her speech was fantastic, and there was no hint of an impediment, usually found with hearing impaired individuals. She was thriving! She was perfect! And then, again, they told me she wasn't. The doctors believed that Lilly actually had a "syndrome."

The first sign of her visual impairment was when I noticed that her right eye was turning in and not following with her other eye. As a person in the medical field, I, of course, jumped to the worst case scenario! In my mind, she had a brain tumor until proven otherwise. Thankfully, and to my utmost relief, it was believed that Lilly had a "lazy eye" and just needed to patch the strong eye until the muscles of the "lazy eye" became stronger. It was decided that she also needed glasses. She was nearly three years old when all of this started to take place. We patched for over a year, first for two hours a day, then three, then four, finally we were patching for eight hours a day without any improvement. I remember that the staff accused me of not really patching. It was allegedly my fault that Lilly wasn't improving. Lilly was miserable when we were patching. She whimpered every time we put her patch on, and she begged us to take it off early, but we wouldn't. How were we to know that she couldn't see out of her right eye, and we were actually making her blind for eight hours a day?

After the ridiculous accusations that we weren't really patching, I finally pressed for more answers. In my heart, I already knew the conclusion, but needed to get us moving in the right direction for a diagnosis. It was determined that Lilly not only had a hearing impairment, but that she was also visually impaired. She had what her doctor called a "central retinal defect" in her right eye, and therefore, patching would never help. Oddly, we actually rejoiced that day because it meant the end of patching, and Lilly was thrilled! She was diagnosed with cone-rod dystrophy in addition to the hearing impairment. Her most likely diagnosis was and still is Usher syndrome. A genetic diagnosis still eludes us.

Usher syndrome is a rare disease in which those who have it slowly become blind and deaf over time. Currently, there is no treatment or cure for Usher syndrome. Of course, the hearing loss can be compensated with hearing aids and eventually a cochlear implant, if the hearing loss reaches the profound range, but the retina of the eye cannot yet be repaired. It can be a devastating disease for the person it affects and those who love them.

When one is given a diagnosis such as Usher syndrome, one can float along in a sea of despair and be a victim, or one can turn the tides in one's favor. Ultimately, happiness is all about one's attitude. Can the diagnosis and all the physical changes be changed? Not likely, but what *can* change is the way one reacts to it. It's important to live life on one's own terms, not on the terms of the diagnosis. Lilly taught me that, not in words, but just by her being.

Lilly was a great baby. She would sleep through anything. (Being hearing impaired has some advantages!) She continues to be the last one up in the morning at sleepovers! She was a happy baby, and her whole body projected her happiness. A light shone from her that could be felt by everyone around her. She was and continues to be an amazing soul. Lilly loves everyone, well… almost. We have a saying, "If Lilly doesn't like you, there is something wrong with YOU." It almost seems as though Lilly can see into a person's soul. She "sees" a person for their true being, not what they project to society. Perhaps her diminished senses make this, so I'm not sure, but I know that everything and everyone look better through Lilly's eyes.

When Lilly was in second grade, at the age of seven, she was instrumental in our family becoming involved with the Foundation Fighting Blindness (FFB). I was checking my email one day, and she was sitting with me. There was an email from FFB inviting us to take part in their signature fundraiser, VisionWalk. We read that email together and she said, "We can do that!" And, so we did!

Lilly discussed her plans with her teacher at school and her second grade class. The class helped us find a team name, and it was appropriately called "Lilly's Friends." We raised $16,000 that year for VisionWalk. Each year since, Lilly and our family have participated in VisionWalk, and we've raised over $150,000 in that time. The money we raise for FFB funds research to find treatments and cures for blinding eye diseases, not just Usher syndrome, but diseases that affect millions of people around the world.

The idea that she could help millions of others as well as possibly herself was incredibly appealing to Lilly. One year, while preparing for VisionWalk, Lilly asked me what it really means to be blind. After I explained it, she asked, "So that's going to happen to me?"

I answered her, "Not if I can help it."

And she said, "OK."

So that's how we left it.

"Not if I can help it." That became my new mantra. This story is about Lilly and how she has changed and inspired those around her. I was changed that day. My resolve was strengthened. Lilly can be who she is because she trusts that my words were true. I am a different person because she makes me want those words to be true. I will stop at nothing to make them so. "For we live by faith, not by sight." (2 Corinthians 5:7) Lilly has faith that everything will be alright. As much as I hate this disease and fear for my daughter's future, I know that everything is going to be alright.

Lilly is twelve now and continues to thrive. She has used her fundraising as a platform to raise awareness for blinding eye diseases like Usher syndrome and encourages others to volunteer as well. Lilly won the prestigious Prudential Spirit of Community Award in 2014, which has led to many other exciting experiences. She was featured in *American Girl* magazine. Lilly was on the *Making a Difference* segment of NBC Nightly News not once, but twice, and has been on local news, as well. Lilly has been on the AOL homepage, and there are many other internet news stories written about her. She gives inspirational speeches to churches, schools, and other groups. Her story is one of success, not only for herself, but also for her cause. She is waging a war on blindness, and as she does so, inspires others to fight their own battles.

Of course, Lilly has her daily struggles. It isn't easy being a twelve-year-old girl with hearing and vision loss. Things that others take for granted are difficult for her, but she rarely complains. She always comes up with a plan B, "a work around," for her struggles. For example, she cannot see the numbers on her locker combination, so she has a lock with a key. She has issues with depth perception, so she grabs someone's hand when she does stairs. The font in her textbooks is too small to read, so she has them on her iPad to increase the font size. There's always another way to get something done. It's all about the attitude. Don't take no for an answer, find the plan B, and make it happen.

It was a beautiful summer day when Lilly was finally diagnosed with her retinal disease. I remember the dress she was wearing, her beautiful blond curls bouncing in the sunshine, and the pink nail polish on her fingernails. My life changed that day. I thought at the time it was for the worse, but it really wasn't. I just didn't know it yet. "The chosen few," that's how I think about Lilly and those like her. This disease called Usher syndrome is so rare, and it can be devastating, but only if you let it. Lilly was chosen, and her life has purpose. She will change the world. She is doing it now.

The summer of her diagnosis, I was devastated. I was in despair. I could not imagine a happy life for my child. I hardly remember what I did from that day until what I call my awakening. That summer my great aunt invited us to her church for a healing service. She explained that her church practiced "laying on of hands" to heal. We are a Christian family, but I can't say I believed something like that would work. The rational side of me, however, thought that it couldn't hurt. My mother, Lilly, and I trekked over to my aunt's church. We met the pastor in the sanctuary, and he prayed over Lilly as I held her. She fell asleep in my arms. He also prayed over me, asking God to heal Lilly of her illness and to mend my broken heart. It was a beautiful, hot, sunny summer day. (The sun always shines when Lilly is around.) I cried my eyes out as we prayed.

Afterward, we went back to my parents' cottage on the lake.

The rest of our family was down at the lake, playing in the water when we returned. We quickly changed into our bathing suits and met them down at the water. Lilly was climbing down the ladder to get in the lake when my father threw a ball for the dog over her head into the water. The dog ran and jumped in, splashing water all over Lilly! She jumped right back up on the dock, spitting and sputtering, hands on her hips and then, pointing a finger at my dad, blond curls tousled by the wind, she said, "That's it! Now I'm mad! You got water all in my eyes and Jesus just fixed them!" I laughed like I had never laughed before. I laughed all the way from my toes. I laughed and laughed and with that laughter, a weight was lifted from me. My soul was lighter than it had been in a very long time. I realized at that exact moment that everything was going to be OK. Our lives were not going to be how I had planned, but we would be fine and Lilly would be fine.

My daughter, Lillian Grace, my Lilly is one of the chosen few. Her eyes may not work how we think they should, but that's okay because Lilly sees through God's eyes. Everything looks better through Lilly's eyes.

ABOUT THE AUTHOR

Angela Diuble grew up and currently resides in Manchester, Michigan, with her husband of twenty years, Scott, their two beautiful and intelligent daughters, Lillian and Abigail, their dog Trixie, and Frankie the Peacock. She is a former high school science teacher and is currently a Physician Assistant practicing in Emergency Medicine.

Angela attended Michigan State University and earned her Bachelor of Arts degree and her teaching certificate from Eastern Michigan University. Angela found her calling in medicine and earned her Master of Science Degree from Medical College of Ohio with a concentration in Physician Assistant Studies.

She has been a devoted fundraiser and the Chairperson for the Michigan VisionWalk for several years and was recently awarded "Volunteer of the Year for the Midwest Region" by the Foundation Fighting Blindness.

Angela likes to spend her free time with the family. She is a huge fan of being at the lake in Northern Michigan, boating, birding, drinking red wine, and perfecting her sarcastic wit. She may even read a book or two now and then.

CHAPTER 2

MY JOURNEY TO AN USHER DIAGNOSIS

A DELAYED DIAGNOSIS PROPELLED THIS AUTHOR INTO POLITICAL ACTIVISM SO OTHERS WOULD NOT HAVE TO WAIT FOR HELP.

LAURA ROUGH

In the 1970s, the United States did not have mandatory newborn hearing testing prior to discharge from the hospital. My hearing problems would go undetected for years. Up to the age of four, I consistently passed my hearing tests despite the fact that my mother and grandma knew I couldn't hear. The audiologists and doctors did not know that they were training me to pass my audiometric test every time by allowing me to study their body language through the window of the audiometric booth (sound booth). It was a fun game for me to catch them and getting the nod of approval. I recall looking through the window of the sound booth from inside and waiting patiently for the shoulder to shrug to tell me to raise my hand because I was not hearing the range of frequencies in my headphone like I was supposed to be able to do. The audiologists would also give that hopeful eye with a gentle smile through the booth window to encourage me to raise my hand, which I did.

Because the medical community did not suspect that I was hard of hearing, but just chose not to hear or behave during the tests, I was thought to be stubborn and to have some behavioral issues. I was placed in the Children Behavior Therapy Unit day program school until they realized that I didn't really have mental issues and that the problem was that I was severely hearing impaired. Thankfully, my grandparents and my mother knew that I was not hearing and didn't give up on me.

When I was four years old, I went to Primary Children's Hospital to see an audiologist, who was able to confirm that I was severely hearing impaired by figuring out that I was actually fooling the previous audiologists. The audiologist came into the sound booth smiling and dropped his pencil on the floor. While he was picking up the pencil, facing away from me, he asked me, "Laura, do you want a cookie?" The audiologist didn't get a response from me except for me smiling. The audiologist asked the same question while facing me. I responded with a bigger smile and nodding yes. It was at that moment that the audiologist realized that I was passing the hearing tests by lip reading and watching through the window for clues as to when to raise my hand during the tests.

During that same visit, the audiologist covered the window to distract me while they were repeating the audiometry test with a range of frequencies going through my headphones. I looked on, wondering if the audiologist was going to ask if I wanted another cookie while I was failing my hearing test. By this time it had taken four years and over twenty doctors finally to find an audiologist that confirmed to my mother that I was profoundly deaf.

I was fit bilaterally with hearing aids shortly after, and with the support of my family, I was on track to start kindergarten in the pubic school system. Along with the other subjects, I had speech therapy during the first seven years of school. I grew up thinking I was the only person with hearing problems, and I never met another deaf or hard of hearing person until I became an adult. The only explanation I was ever given was that my hearing impairment was due to nerve damage.

In 1995 while in college, I began to notice subtle changes in my vision, but I couldn't pinpoint what it was. It was going to the local cave in Utah that made me think something had changed. I remembered going there as a child, and I was able to see inside the cave; now I was not able to see because of the dim lighting. I was also running into objects and people that I didn't see. It seemed puzzling to me that I was able to see my friends and the chairs in the movie theater when I was in high school, but I was not able to see people, faces, or chairs in the movie theaters in my twenties.

Over the years, eye tests showed that I was farsighted and needed glasses, but nothing else was abnormal. Since I was concerned about the changes, the ophthalmologist did the Goldmann perimeter test that checked for peripheral vision loss. I was instructed to look into the center of the globe and push a button when I saw the red dot. The tech kept repeating that I had to push the button when I saw the red dot during the test. I kept telling the tech that I was pushing the button when I saw the dots. The tech kept repeating, "I know you saw that!" Meanwhile I was thinking to myself, "Why am I not seeing the dots?" Sadly, the technician concluded that my test was normal. This conclusion didn't stop me from getting another opinion.

Sadly, this brought back memories for my mother of my passing my hearing tests although I was hard of hearing. Once again, the medical community was missing something, and now it had to do with my vision. I was given the suggestion to go see a psychiatrist, since the problem may have all been in my head.

Because the technician passed me on the most important test, I went down the route to ruling out other medical diagnoses with a lumbar puncture, but I was still at a loss since there were still no answers to the vision issues. I later scheduled an appointment with a neuro-ophthalmologist at the Moran Eye Center in Salt Lake City, Utah, for a full day of testing. At the end of the testing, a retina specialist came in to look into my eyes. He put his hand on my knee to tell me that I had *retinitis pigmentosa* (RP), but that this could also be Usher syndrome. The doctor added, "Laura, you are losing you vision." Amazingly, twenty more years had passed since the hearing loss diagnosis. Years later it would be confirmed through blood work as Usher syndrome type 2A.

Finding out that I was going blind was the hardest part, since I had grown up being hard of hearing and found comfort saying to myself that I would always have my vision. Now, I tell myself that at least I am alive to enjoy another day, taking life one day at a time, and trying not to focus on the unknown.

I was never crazy nor did I have behavioral problems, and it took the medical community a while to figure out that this smart girl had learned how to lip read and study body language to pass her hearing tests as a young child. Since I didn't look or behave as if I were blind, it took years until the right specialists were able to confirm that I had *retinitis pigmentosa* as part of Usher syndrome. Being stubborn also helped me keep moving forward to prove who I was.

As I grow older, I have found that managing life with Usher syndrome is about getting the right resources and training to continue to live independently. Quite often to secure these services we have to advocate for ourselves and let our legislators know where we stand. That is what I had to do on January 27, 2010, when I spoke in front of the legislators in the Senate building about the implications of the state of Utah's threat to reduce the budget by cutting the budget to the Blind Center/Vocational Rehabilitation. I explained to them how valuable the Division of Services for the Blind and Visually Impaired had been for me. Their programs allowed me to finish Nursing School and complete my RN degree. I added that with their continued support and training, I had been able to maintain employment as a Nurse Case Manager at the University Healthcare Hospital.

After outlining the services the Division for the Blind and Visually Impaired provided, including mobility training and Daily Living Skills classes, I wanted the legislators to realize that I was one of many blind/visually impaired people who relied on these services. To do so I stated that if they wanted to save money for the Utah budget, they needed to add more funding for blind services, not reduce it. These services allow thousands of people who are facing blindness to maintain their careers and keep earning taxable income rather than drawing social security. In fact, there are studies proving that these programs pay for themselves many times over. The budget cut was saved, and many more blind/visually impaired people have continued to benefit from the services that have helped them to further their education and get the needed training to remain in the workforce as long as possible.

ABOUT THE AUTHOR

Laura Rough is a first generation college graduate in her family and fulfilled her dream of being a Registered Nurse. She currently works at a hospital in the Case Management Office. When she is not working, one will find Laura pausing from time to time with her camera to capture pictures "through Laura's eyes" and sharing on social media the beauty everyone can see all around while she is losing her vision. Laura was the hostess for the 2015 RP (*retinitis pigmentosa*) Social, an annual event that takes place somewhere in the U.S. or Canada. The purpose of the RP Social is to get people together, make new friends, and network with others who have RP or Usher syndrome. She continues to advocate for services for the blind/visually impaired and the deaf in Utah. Laura resides in Salt Lake City, Utah, with her husband Erik Jorgensen.

CHAPTER 3

MY LITTLE SECRET

THE CHALLENGE... AND STRESS... OF HIDING USHER FROM FAMILY AND FRIENDS. EARLY ONSET BLINDNESS AT AGE 22.

RANDI KNUTSON

I was a sophomore and having a blast playing volleyball for Catonsville (Maryland) High School. The Comets were having an amazing season and were ready to take on the next team! One autumn afternoon, we were bused to our competitor's gym for what I believed to be an easy game. Already dressed in our uniforms, we headed into the gym to do our warm-ups. I remember feeling disoriented because the gymnasium looked like a dreary storm cloud, and I immediately became nervous. I did not understand the anxiety at the time, but I no longer felt sure of this game.

I started in the right corner of the court, which was my spike position. The ball was served to our side of the court, our center bumped the ball to our setter, and then she began to set the ball for me to spike. A simple play and one of my favorites! I watched the ball go up, and then I tried to follow its path and lost it. It was not lost for long because what goes up must come down. The ball did just that. It came down on my head!

As a teenager, my peripheral vision was beginning to narrow, night blindness was setting in, and visual adjustments were quite time-consuming, with adjusting from daylight to darkness and vice-versa. My eyes did not want to cooperate with me and felt like they were becoming my enemy. My partial deafness had already brought endless teasing, ongoing bullying, and kids generally making me an outcast. I was determined that I was not going to have blindness to further alienate me, and therefore, no one was allowed to know what was going on. I was willing to make sacrifices. I was going to do what it took to protect this secret of mine, not understanding its cost. I was going to need a whole lot of excuses, miss out on opportunities, and unintentionally hurt my family and friends.

Losing my peripheral vision meant that oftentimes I might not see the person a few feet away waving her hands to get my attention. To further complicate matters, my eyeballs would make direct contact with a person, but I still could not see them. I could never defend against the gossip about me becoming a snob or simply being rude. I truly could not see them. I did not believe there was anything that I could do to change that.

When I started to experience night blindness, I became afraid of how I would act around others in the midst of the darkness, instead of what dangers might be lurking around in the night. I made plenty of excuses as to why I could not be out after dark. It was rather easy since I was a teenager living at home. There were times that I knew I had been caught not being able to see well in the dark.

One day, I was volunteering for a local food ministry, and we were going to be making a home delivery. The elderly lady lived off a gravel road deep in the woods and did not have any of her outside lights turned on! Needless to say, it did not matter how slowly I walked, I still tripped onto the deck. Thankfully I did not hurt myself, anyone else, or the groceries.

One beautiful spring morning, I took a walk to a community blood drive. It was not my first time donating blood, but it was my first time going to this building. Once I was inside, I needed time to allow my eyes to make their adjustment from outdoors daylight to being indoors. I was immediately nervous because I could feel the tension surrounding me while I stood in a corner of a church doorway. When I was able to make my way through the church, I was still very anxious because I was paranoid about walking into a person, or worse, knocking over a table full of supplies. They summoned me to a booth for a quick interview and physical. My heart rate was a little high. Actually, it was really high to the point that I was told that I was not allowed to donate blood on that day. I kept trying to tell myself to relax, but it was not working. I left that morning, feeling sad and disappointed in myself. My little secret was interfering with my ability to help someone else.

I remember the pivotal moment that my *retinitis pigmentosa* (RP) could no longer be my little secret. It was in the late afternoon hour, and I was waiting for my ride to pick me up from work. They pulled into the parking lot, and I went to the car to get into its passenger seat. However, there was a problem. I did not open the door to the correct car. The ladies in the wrong car looked terrified! I still remember the look on the elderly lady's face to this day. Owing to that particular experience, I realized I could not hide my *retinitis pigmentosa* or deny what was going on to others. I had to find answers.

HUNT FOR ANSWERS

My mom had had enough. She scheduled an eye appointment for us to discuss what was wrong with my vision. She was unsuccessful in getting me to talk about it because "it was my little secret." Everyone else did not believe that there was something wrong with my vision. They thought I was too lazy to watch where I was going, or that I had stopped caring about others even to the point of not acknowledging their waves.

My first, second, third, fourth, and many other appointments with a local optometrist generally were the same exams with the same results, and they did not yield any answers as to what was wrong with my vision. There were times when I felt as though there was no answer as to what was happening to my vision. I prayed that I would meet a doctor who would believe me, even if he did not have the answers to this mysterious journey.

There was one doctor visit that I will never forget. Someone suggested that I should try going to see an eye doctor at the Katzen Eye Group. On the day of my appointment, I met with the nurse tech first. He explained to me how I was to push a button every time I saw one of the LED lights come on. It was a field test.

The machine is large, and it reminded me of a bull's eye with a ring of LED lights and one LED light in the center. I had to stare at the center LED light as the tech would randomly turn on one of the other lights within the circle. I was supposed to push the button every time I saw that light.

It was strange because I never saw those lights. I kept my focus on that center LED light and never saw any of the surrounding LED lights. I felt as though I was doing something wrong. At the end of the test, the nurse tech came into the room and asked as to why I never pushed the button. I explained that I never saw any of the other LED lights come on. He proceeded to check the machine to see if it was malfunctioning. It seemed to be working properly, and then he stated that I would need to take the test again. I took the test for a second time, and the end result was the same: I did not see any of the lights come on. The nurse tech returned to the exam room and asked if I understood how I was to take the test and when to push the button. Even though I replied that I knew what I was supposed to do, he felt the need to explain the directions again. I took the field test a third time, with the same results as the two previous tests.

I was moved out of the exam room and switched to a standard doctor's office, where I waited to speak with the optometrist. After she came in, we discussed my reasoning for the eye appointment and all of the issues that I had been having the past several years. We discussed the field test results, which were blank and did not make sense to her, how I could completely fail the exam three different times. She stated that she noticed that I was wearing two hearing aids and wanted to make sure that I understood how to take the test and when to push the button. Even though I had already explained that I did, in fact, understand, my word was apparently not satisfactory. She insisted that I share with her in my own words how I was to take the test. I did so, and she was still puzzled. Her questioning then took a different direction. It was not about my vision, but rather, what family life was like at home or if I had ever felt depressed. At this point, I stopped believing that she came into work that morning with the intention of listening or helping her patients.

It did not stop there, though. She kept dwelling on my hearing aids and continued to question whether or not I was capable of following directions. She asked me to complete a few simple tasks. I bet you saw this coming, right? I had to stand with my left leg while holding my right foot and vice versa. I also had to extend both arms out to my side and when directed, touch my nose with my left index finger and vice versa. "Okay, Doc! I am not depressed, and my family is wanting answers as much as I do, so quit talking to me as if I am stupid, pretending that you care, and tell me what is wrong!!"

Unfortunately, she could not hear me yelling at her with my mind. I left her office with her recommendation for me to speak with a psychiatrist, which so happened to be on a different floor of this particular building. All I wanted to do was leave and never look back. I purposely waited until my aunt and I left the office before telling her the outcome of my appointment. If I had relayed the events with the doctor to my aunt before we left the office, let's just say that I would be writing an entirely, different ending to this experience.

I shared my previous experience with a dear co-worker of mine. She knew an optometrist who was very personable and thorough with all of his patients. I met with Dr. Benjamin Hedin and could have hugged the man to death! There was finally a doctor that not only believed what I had been experiencing, but also understood my condition to be *retinitis pigmentosa*. He gave me a referral to go to Wilmer Eye Institute at Johns Hopkins Hospital in Baltimore for my final diagnosis of Usher syndrome type 2, leading me to my next series of adventures.

ADVENTURES IN SHADES

At Wilmer Eye Institute at Johns Hopkins Hospital, I was diagnosed as legally blind due to Usher syndrome type 2. I had spent several years keeping it a secret, and then spent a year hunting down an answer. What was I to do next? A lady that worked for the county school district as a student advocate for the deaf and hearing impaired suggested that I seek training. That is exactly what I did. Division of Rehabilitation Services found a program that would teach me how to travel with a white cane, learn to read braille, use adaptive technology, and live independently. All that I needed to do was to quit my job and commit the next nine months to a new way of living. As a twenty year old, I was willing to take on the challenge and ready for an adventure!

The program that I was taking part in believed in using sleep shades to help a legally blind person truly understand how to live as a totally blind individual. That meant wearing these shades for eight hours a day, five days a week. My classmates and I all lived in a co-ed dormitory apartment and were all there for different reasons. Most were legally blind with a variety of causes for their blindness, while a few others were totally blind. Regardless of our background and what brought all of us together, we became a family and truly leaned on each other for support as we embraced this new journey.

The most challenging class that I had to take was my cane travel class. It was not necessarily scary for me, but it was for my family and friends. They seemed to be a little uneasy about a young girl walking around a big city while wearing black sleep shades and using a white cane. I grew up in the country, so I was not familiar with city life, but I was able to hold my own. It continues to amaze me to this day, how the first people to offer me assistance were the ones who were considered to be lower class, like the homeless, drug dealers, and street walkers. They never asked me for anything. They only wanted to help me get to my destination.

There were a lot of prayers for me while I was in training. I know it to be true, for I witnessed many miracles. One afternoon, I was going out on a trip for my cane travel class. I came to a traffic light and waited for the light to turn red so that I could cross the two-lane road and then catch the bus. I would know it was time to cross the street by listening to the street traffic. The cars in front of me had all come to a stop, and that meant it was safe for me to cross, or so I thought. When I reached the middle of the street, I heard two men yelling out, "Stop! Stop!" I did as they said and stopped in the middle of the street. A split second later, I learned why they were yelling at me to stop. A tractor trailer came flying past me, and the wind draft from the truck pushed me back a few paces.

Once the trailer disappeared, I quickly finished crossing the street. The two men who had yelled for me to stop came over to check on me. I could not believe that I had misjudged the traffic pattern and nearly died. The men reassured me that I had timed it correctly, and that the tractor trailer had run through the red light. I have not shared the best part of the story yet. Those two men were working on a six-month construction project. They always worked the morning shift; however, on this day a machine was not working properly, and their schedule had been rearranged to work that particular afternoon. That was the first and only time that I saw those men.

For each of our classes, we had to complete final projects in order to graduate. For instance, our independent living class wanted us to be able to prepare meals for a small gathering of four to six guests, as well as to plan a party for a minimum of twenty-five guests. All the shopping, preparation, cooking, setup, and cleanup had to be done without any assistance. The braille and computer classes had us take final exams to showcase what we had learned throughout the year. Our cane travel class dropped us off. Yes, they dropped us off as part of our final project. The instructors drove around in many circles to confuse our location, and then dropped us off. We were then expected to find our way back to the school. There were two stipulations though. First, we were only allowed to ask a yes or no question. Additionally, we were only allowed to ask up to three people. The instructors were following us from a distance to ensure there was no cheating. There were a total of three drop-off routes, and if you did not make it back to the school within a reasonable amount of time, then it did not count. The second aspect of their final project involved us having to use three different forms of transportation to go to a new destination. For instance, I took the bus to the light rail, light rail to the airport, and then took a plane to Miami.

The odd part to my training was that I had drastically lost my sight. As I mentioned earlier, we had to wear the sleep shades five days a week, for eight hours a day. I was not the only person who had similar experiences. Many students experienced the same vision issues prior to my class and after our graduating the class. All of us had a progressive disease, but not the same type of condition. I truly believe that it is the cause for my current state, which is total blindness at the age of thirty-four. Regardless of the reasoning, I would not have been able to do the things that I do and live independently, without the proper training that I received.

ABOUT THE AUTHOR

(Randi Knutson, second from right)

Randi Knutson is 34 years of age and calls Catonsville, Maryland, her hometown.

As a toddler, she was not able to speak clearly. The family doctor thought he could cure the problem by clipping underneath her tongue. To the doctor's surprise, it did not correct her speech impediment! Her determined mom, however, noticed that she would not always react to the sounds around her. Eventually, Randi had a hearing test and by age three, began wearing two hearing aids. She became legally blind in late 2000 due to Usher syndrome type 2. Her condition rapidly declined within a short time frame, and she is now fully blind with mild balance issues.

Randi's time is filled with a range of responsibilities, such as marketing for a non-profit organization the past nine years, annual mission trips throughout the country, and being on the receiving end of a helpline for those late night computer hiccups.

"God gave me strength and courage to live a blessed, independent life," she says. "He was also generous enough to surround me with inspirational parents, devoted sisters, unwavering family members, and obnoxious friendships. I thank God and I thank all of those who are dear to my heart for allowing me to be a part of their lives."

CHAPTER 4

LIFE WITH A LATE USHER DIAGNOSIS

A NATIVE OF MADRID, SPAIN, THIS AUTHOR'S USHER
CONDITION WENT UNDETECTED FOR YEARS BECAUSE SHE WAS
SO GOOD AT COPING. EDUCATED IN THE UK AND THE US, SHE
CONTINUES TO INSPIRE WITH HER MANY ACHIEVEMENTS.

MARISA HERRERA POSTLEWATE, PHD

Would a child be better off not knowing that he/she has Usher syndrome? Should one even bother to get a diagnosis if there is no treatment? While there is no right or wrong answer, every child deserves an equal opportunity to excel and receive the education that can best prepare him/her for a productive adult life. The following vignettes are little glimpses into the past of a child growing up without a diagnosis of Usher syndrome and how she adapted to live a "normal" life.

HEARING LOSS

I remember when I was a young adult knitting with my grandmother. She shared stories of my early years that now make me wonder if my hearing loss was evident even before my first diagnosis of a mild hearing loss at age 12. She described me as a quiet, pensive child who often sat for long periods in deep thought and unaware of the surroundings. She predicted I would be a philosopher, and she was close because I eventually earned a Doctor of Philosophy (PhD) in Spanish Literature.

There were times when I would be in the living area of our small apartment with a long hallway when my aunt would call me to open the door. Only when my great-grandfather who was in the same room yelled at me would I get up and go open the door. Did I not hear my aunt calling me or was I just being rebellious? One thing is certain—Spanish people speak louder than Americans, so one would have to have moderate-to-severe hearing loss before anyone would suspect a hearing problem or recommend hearing aids.

My younger sister, Juana, always wanted to share "secrets," especially while in bed, and I couldn't make out her whispers unless I could read her lips. If I couldn't see her mouth, I couldn't "hear" her, and the hearing problem was made more pronounced by the absence of light.

I was easily startled even when I knew there were other people around me. When someone I didn't see spoke, I would jump and scream, often uncontrollably. It became a game with my siblings and some of my classmates. In fact, I was sent to the principal's office more than once for screaming in the hallway. I tried to explain to him that I just could not help it. I don't think he believed me, but I never got detention and instead was just told to try to control myself. My peers would try to surprise me every chance they got, and I never understood why I was so jumpy. Looking back, it was obvious that I did not hear or see the person in the room. I continue to be jumpy even today. My husband will usually clear his throat when he is around me as a warning, in case I don't see or hear him.

Other than being diagnosed with mild hearing loss, my years in primary and secondary school were uneventful, and my hearing was not an issue. However, consciously or subconsciously, I always tried to sit on the window side of the classroom and close to the front to minimize glare issues, so I could see the board and hear what was being said around me. Large college classes, often held in an auditorium-style lecture hall, were somewhat problematic. I wasn't the only one having difficulties in the lecture halls, so I didn't think much about it. I always studied with other classmates, and we would compare notes and fill in the gaps.

Studying French in college proved to be a challenge, especially when it came to the oral part. Perhaps it was because I did a lot of lip reading. Anyone who has seen a person speaking French knows it is practically impossible to read their lips. I could not understand why I had such difficulty since I had learned English as a young teen. My first English teacher claimed I intimidated her because I was like a sponge mastering the assignments quickly, and always wanting to learn more. I remember talking to the French Conversation professor about this issue during my junior year. Her solution to my difficulty with the pronunciation and deciphering what was being said was to put my hair, which was straight and down to my waist, behind the ears in order to hear better. Now, why didn't I think of that innovative idea? Needless to say, the professor's suggestion didn't work, but I made it through the course and decided that a minor in French was all I needed.

EYESIGHT

I have always been extremely sensitive to sunlight, even as a small child. During my youth, most photographs were taken outdoors. In those photographs, I was always squinting, frowning, or rubbing my eyes. In many photos when I was as young as two, I look like I just didn't get my way and was on the verge of tears. I really think it was my reaction to the sunlight sensitivity. I got prescription reading glasses at the age of eight, even though my visual acuity was close to 20/20. I recall the only reason I got them was that I had recurring headaches. I was told that I had to get glasses because I had big eyes. It is true that my eyes are big, so I believed it. Getting my eyes checked was an annual routine from that point onward.

At age 18, I passed the driver's test, including the vision test and the visual-field test. When I was about 20, I told the ophthalmologist that I saw constant flashes in front of my eyes, and he replied that it was common in people with astigmatism. Since I had astigmatism, I just accepted it. He recommended that I wear tinted or transition lenses. The latter helped while I was outdoors, but they never lightened fast enough once I went indoors. I opted for prescription sunglasses in addition to regular glasses.

When I was about 40, the eye doctor dilated my eyes to check the developing cataracts. It was then that he saw some pigmentation and sent me to a retina specialist. He told me that I had what looked like early stages of *retinitis pigmentosa* (RP) due to the subtle pigmentation present. The doctor gave me no real explanation, but I knew a little about it because my brother had been diagnosed with RP in his 30s. I wasn't concerned because I didn't think it was affecting my daily life, so I did no further research. Years later I learned that I was probably legally blind, or close to it, when diagnosed, but the doctors never shared that information with me.

SITUATIONS IN THE DARK

Anyone familiar with RP knows that one of its first signs is night blindness or difficulty seeing in dimly lit places. Walking at night along Madrid's main streets when growing up was not a problem. There was plenty of street lighting, and the stores all left the window display lights on so that people could window-shop even after closing. However, I do remember slamming right into a tree in the city's large El Retiro Park when I was in my twenties. I was walking on the paved area with my aunt and my cousin's little boy, who was enthusiastically showing me all the area's highlights. He had me looking from one side to the other and before I knew it, I was off the sidewalk. I turned right into a tree and my glasses went flying off my face. The little boy picked up my broken glasses from the ground, and my aunt reprimanded him for distracting me so much that I had a hard time seeing where I was walking. Thinking back, I wonder if my aunt noticed that something was wrong with my vision, or if she was simply trying to slow down a hyperactive child. In any event, that incident left me wondering why such a thing could happen to me and nobody else. Do people really have to make a conscious effort to concentrate on their surroundings when walking?

It's true that most children are scared of the dark and eventually outgrow it, but I didn't. I still get nervous in the dark, even in familiar surroundings. As a child and young teen, I lived on the fourth floor of an apartment building in Madrid. I can remember running up or down each flight of stairs and hitting the timed-light button to make sure the power always stayed on. Once on my floor, I would hit every light button down the long hallway. By the time I reached the destination inside or outside of the building, my heart would be beating very rapidly.

At the age of nine I was chosen to go to a summer camp for one week, which was my first time away from home on my own. It was at a military-type camp up in the mountains outside of Madrid where we marched a lot. I was among the tallest campers, so I always followed others. With that advantage, I don't recall having trouble getting around even though it was a rather dark and bare looking place. I was assigned a top bunk in a large room with lots of bunk beds lined up on both sides. The first night at camp, I fell and hit myself on the bunk next to mine, cutting my earlobe. I had no idea where the light switch was, and I didn't dare to move because it was totally dark and I could not see. I just sat there crying until the girls around me woke up and someone turned on the light. My earlobe was bleeding, and the chaperone came and gave me lots of cloth handkerchiefs to stop the bleeding. From that night on, I made sure I didn't move while in bed, not even to roll over.

At home, my sister Juana, who had no vision problems, loved to turn the light off on me and hear me scream uncontrollably to the point that it became an almost daily game for her. At bedtime she would wait for me around the corner and as I reached the top of the stairs, she would say, "Boo!" I knew it was coming, yet I could not refrain from screaming. Darkness was such a fear that for many years I had a recurring dream that I was stuck in an endless, dark hallway and could not find my way out.

Going to the movies in Madrid was not a problem because there were ushers who would guide you to an assigned seat with a flashlight. That changed when we came to the United States. I adapted by making sure that I got to my seat before the lights were dimmed. Going to dances was somewhat stressful, but I stood or sat wherever there seem to be more light, and I avoided very dark locales. As a young high school teacher, I had to chaperone a lot of dances. I would stand by the door to have a wide view that allowed me to keep an eye on the kids better. The disco lights gave enough light for me to figure out what was going on in the room.

It's hard to tell when I started having problems seeing in the dark. I do remember that I could not see well in totally dark areas, unlike my sister and mother, but I just thought everyone was different. As long as there was some light, I seemed to do well. I have to admit, though, that daylight was and is my favorite time when outdoors. It's like my personality changes after dark, and I would walk slower and become quieter in order to concentrate on what's around me.

COMPENSATING FOR VISUAL FIELD LOSS

As far back as I can remember, adult family members would tell me to walk straight and hold my head up. I thought I was walking like everyone else. Apparently I walked looking at the ground in front of my feet, which is probably what most people with RP will do in order to avoid obstacles. Nobody suspected the posture issue was related to my vision. Instead, the family doctor thought I was growing too fast and suggested to my mom that I start wearing a training bra! Well, it didn't help my posture, and they continued to tell me to walk straight long after I stopped growing.

Walking with a group of people was often comical unless I was holding on to someone. Let's just say that I started doing the "bump" long before the dance was in style. I always seemed to bump into those next to me or step on the heels of those walking in front. I either couldn't see them or misjudged our exact locations. My solution was to walk a few steps behind to be able to see the people and avoid bumping into them. I still do this even today when not holding on to someone's arm. I remember friends asking why I always walked behind them instead of next to them. I just told them that I didn't know why. I told them it was easier for me to walk that way when in a group, and it had nothing to do with how I felt about the people whom I walked with.

Being the oldest of five, with two siblings eleven and thirteen years younger than I, there were always toys and other things lying around. One of the most vivid memories is a Christmas when my little brother got the latest remote-controlled airplane from our aunt and uncle. That novel plane never had the chance to fly because I came walking into the living room and, not seeing the toy, I found it with my feet, crushing it. I couldn't understand what had happened because I did not see anything in my path. Earlier that day, my stepfather and I bumped into each other as he was coming around the corner into the living room. I thought he was the one who didn't see me. On that famous Christmas day, I was called a few not-so-pleasant names that would stay with me for many years. I just didn't understand why the adults thought I was careless by not watching where I was going. I was a fast walker, but I sure thought I was watching my every step. If we had known something wasn't working quite right with my eyes, someone would have warned me about the plane or would have placed the plane out of my path, and my stepfather would have been on the lookout. I certainly would have been spared from feeling like a big, clumsy teen that deep down I knew I was not.

CHOOSING A CAREER

I had many career interests, including nursing, computer programming, and being an interpreter for the United Nations. The latter was the first one scratched because I didn't think my hearing was good enough. The other two were eliminated for reasons unrelated to Usher syndrome symptoms. I had not thought of teaching as a career, but halfway through my sophomore year in college, I had the opportunity to team-teach a second-semester Spanish class. Everything went well in spite of my mild hearing loss, and my visual-field loss was not an issue yet. My professors encouraged me to become a Spanish teacher and use the language tools I already had.

After the first few years as a teacher, I found myself rearranging the classroom so that I could have most or all students within my visual field. In spite of doing this, I still thought that my visual field was like that of everyone else. I found that as the years passed I would rearrange the desks closer and closer together. A good portion of the rectangular-shaped room would go unused while my students occupied what seemed like a square. With the smaller classes, I would arrange them in a semi-circle. Even with such arrangements I would often scan to see if anyone had their hand up to ask questions. This was tiring, so I set rules that no questions were to be asked until the question/answer period following the lecture. I didn't think that what I was doing had anything to do with my vision and nobody complained, so I didn't see it as anything unusual. Looking back, I see that it was a way of adapting to my visual-field limitations. If I was using overhead projectors, if I was showing a film, or if there was a power-point presentation, I would open some of the blinds so that there was enough light for me to see what was going on. I always made sure the path to the light switch was free of obstacles. At one point I put a string of clear Christmas lights around the blackboards so there was always some extra light. The students loved it, and I had the light I needed. I never sat at my desk and would instead move around the classroom always trying to be close to the student who was asking or answering a question, probably to make sure I could hear him/her. I continued to do this even after I started wearing hearing aids.

I also found myself implementing other rules that would make my navigation through the classroom easier. The backpacks were to be under the desks to keep the aisles clear. Students were to sharpen pencils at the beginning of class, and everyone was to remain seated until the bell rang or I instructed them to do otherwise. These are ways to keep everyone safe, but the unusual visual field was probably a reason why I needed a more structured setting.

CONCLUSION

What I want the reader to take away from this writing is that a late diagnosis with RP/Usher is not necessarily because there are no signs, but because, as in my case, I was able to compensate, and the doctors were obviously not familiar with the disorder. Does this mean that a later diagnosis is synonymous to later development of Usher syndrome? It is a genetic disorder, so it is present, however subtle, from birth. Having good visual acuity helped me to compensate for visual-field loss, and being a good lip reader helped compensate for the hearing loss. Being seen as a clumsy, careless teen because of my bumping into relatives that were in front of my eyes and stepping on things in my path affected me emotionally. I eventually convinced myself that it didn't matter what anyone else thought because I knew what they were saying was not true.

Now that doctors are more familiar with Usher syndrome and assistive technology is much more advanced, an early diagnosis enables the individual to search out available tools early on. I could probably have benefited from hearing aids at a younger age, but the analog technology amplified all sounds equally so that the sound of pages turning was as loud as someone's voice. Today's digital technology has taken care of those problems and makes everything sound as it would sound normally. I would encourage parents to become familiar with the technology that could help their affected children to be successful like others and always expect the best they can do given their limitations. Do not force accommodations, but let the child decide when it's time, as long as he/she is not struggling. There are many faces to Usher syndrome and, as in life, there is no single correct path to follow.

ABOUT THE AUTHOR

Dr. Marisa Herrera Postlewate was clinically diagnosed with RP in 1994, and it was confirmed through genetic testing as USH2A in 2013. A native of Madrid, Spain, she holds a B.A. from the University of Maine, an M.A. from New York University/University of Salamanca (Spain) program, and a PhD from the University of Texas at Arlington. She retired from the University of Texas at Arlington after 25 years in education. Marisa is a published author of literary criticism and translations of various genres. She has also translated several websites including those of the Usher Syndrome Coalition and Leader Dogs for the Blind. She currently lives in Texas with her husband and continues to write, volunteer in her community, and travel throughout the United States, Spain, and Latin America. In 2010 she had Orientation and Mobility training through Leader Dogs for the Blind in Rochester, Michigan.

PART 2

LIFE IN AN USHER FAMILY

CHAPTER 5

FEARING THE UNKNOWN

A MOTHER TALKS ABOUT THE DIFFICULTIES ADOPTING A CHILD
AS AN USHER PARENT, RAISING TWO CHILDREN, AND LEARNING
TO LIVE LIFE TO ITS FULLEST.

ANNA SENGILLO

I was diagnosed with Usher syndrome at the age of 26. I experienced night blindness as a teenager, but I believed this was normal. I remember having some difficulty driving at night especially when I made a turn into a front yard instead of the adjacent street. There were many incidents like this, and I just shrugged them off and attributed them to not being able to see well at night.

It was in my twenties that I noticed some peripheral vision changes. One day while at work, the top drawer of a tall filing cabinet was fully opened. While looking down, I walked towards the cabinet. The file drawer was opened at eye level, and I walked right into it, with my face smashing against the metal edges. At that moment I realized I needed to make an appointment with my eye doctor to figure out why I did not see the file drawer. I was convinced I had glaucoma because my father had the disease.

After the examination, my ophthalmologist referred me to a retina specialist because he saw some bone *spicules* in the mid-periphery of the retina. I became alarmed and frightened. It wasn't glaucoma. The retina specialist said, "You have Usher syndrome." He gave me a pamphlet from Foundation Fighting Blindness and sent me on my way. He did not explain what Usher syndrome was or what to expect. I was scared and lost. What did this mean? Was I going blind? I didn't know anything about Usher syndrome, but I learned as time went on.

I continued to drive, since I was not legally blind at 26. At 31, I gave up my license. It was at this time that my husband and I were thinking of possibly starting a family. Because there was so little known about Usher syndrome at the time, I did not want to have a biological child for fear of passing on the disease. It took us a year to finally come to the decision to adopt. I did not know if I would be able to raise children as a mother with Usher syndrome. How would I be able to "see" them grow? How would I be able to keep them safe? Would I hear their cries? Would I be able to hear them call my name in the middle of the night? Would my eyes worsen before they were old enough to care for themselves?

The fears and concerns of raising a child while being blind and hearing impaired consumed me. This led me to make a trip to see a prominent retina specialist in Houston, Texas. I needed confirmation that I would not go blind. He reassured me that I would have functional vision at 50, and encouraged me to go ahead with our plans for adoption. I still remember his words: "Blind people can raise children!"

My husband and I left Houston with a sense of peace and confidence to continue with the adoption process. Within six months, we were matched with a beautiful Korean girl. She was two months old when our caseworker presented a picture of her to us. My husband and I were so excited and fell in love with her the minute we saw her photo. I immediately started to plan, decorate, and pick out colors for her bedroom! We named her Candice, and we couldn't wait to hold her in our arms.

The adoption almost did not take place. The caseworker from the adoption agency called my husband and explained to him that the director of the Korean adoption agency was about to deny Candice coming to America to be placed in our home. My husband was told that the director did not want to have Candice placed in a home with a deafblind mother raising her. I was at work when this conversation took place and not aware of the phone call to my husband.

Our caseworker instructed my husband to get a letter from my eye doctor stating I would not go blind. My husband was furious and became worried! He called the retina specialist we had seen in Houston and told him that we were being denied the adoption because of my eye disease. The retina specialist made a call to Korea and spoke directly to the director of the Korean adoption agency. He reprimanded him for the denial and informed him that I was perfectly able to raise and care for Candice. My husband kept this whole incident from me until after Candice was in our home. The director of the Korean adoption agency granted us the adoption of Candice after speaking with the retina specialist, whom I would call our "angel."

When Candice was placed in my arms, at the age of four months, I no longer thought about having Usher syndrome. My focus was to care and love her. What I did have to do was think of how I could make sure she was kept safe.

LIFE AS AN USHER MOTHER

When she was an infant I always cupped my hand over her head when navigating around my home, especially through doorways and narrow passages. Her room was decorated with bright colors and bright lighting to help me see better. When she was ready for the walker, my home became a barricade haven. We had baby gates everywhere, and I basically confined her to two rooms in which to navigate in the walker. Every outlet was baby-proofed with safety plugs. There were no objects lying around that I could miss seeing her getting her hands on.

At bedtime, while she was asleep, I would have the baby monitor at the head of my bed attached to the headboard and volume on high. That way I could hear her cry without my hearing aids. I could not hear her breathe, so that's where I relied on my husband's hearing. Our days were filled with fun, and she kept me busy! We lived in a quiet neighborhood, so taking her for a walk in the stroller around the cul-de-sac became a daily outing.

Six months after our daughter arrived, I found out I was pregnant with our son Jesse. I never wanted Candice to be an only child, but I feared passing on the Usher gene to a biological child. I believed this was God's way of saying, "You can do this," but I was still afraid. Two kids 18 months apart! How was I going to be able to do this with my deteriorating eyesight? Our daughter would only be a year and a half old when our son Jesse was born.

After Jesse was born, my fears resurfaced. Did I pass on the Usher gene to him? Despite the fact that the retina specialist from Houston explained to my husband and me that there would be a one in four hundred chance that a biological child would be affected, I was concerned and became anxious. He explained to us we would notice hearing loss in Jesse very early on as a child. When Jesse was an infant, I would enter his room while he was sleeping in his crib. The bedroom door had a faint creaking sound when opened. I wanted to check his response to the sound. I would sometimes clap lightly and was happy to see his little head pop up. He could hear! I continued to do these little tests to make sure there wasn't a change. I found out later in a conversation with my husband that he was doing the same thing! Jesse did not have Usher syndrome, but he would be a carrier.

Candice was a good toddler and didn't demand my constant attention, so caring for Jesse was not as stressful. They became close playmates and loved playing together. Jesse, however, was more curious and would get into things. Candice somehow knew that I could not see well and would alert me when Jesse got himself into trouble.

I remember one day while I was talking on the phone, Jesse was walking around in his walker. I had forgotten to secure the baby gate, and he snuck past me. He went into the foyer, which led to a two-step sunken living room. He flipped over upside down as he went down the steps! I did not hear or see him go by. He did not cry, but Candice immediately came running to tell me that he had fallen down! She was only two years old, and I remember the frightened look on her face. Jesse was not hurt, but this incident really shook me up. It reminded me to never forget to put that gate up. I had to be more diligent baby-proofing the house with Jesse around!

Both my children learned very early that I could not see well and had no peripheral vision. My central vision at that time was very good. When Jesse was two years old, he would play little jokes on me. He would hide things and take away a diaper that was nearby when I was about to change him. He would laugh when I was not able to locate it! Both children eventually became my little helpers, and when I needed help locating an object, they were eager to show me where it was.

Jesse was more than helpful when my husband and I would go grocery shopping. For a while neither of us could figure out some of the purchases we had made when we unpacked our groceries at home. Both of us were convinced the other had put the items in the shopping cart. Finally, one day my husband witnessed Jesse, who was sitting in the cart, reaching out and pulling random items off the shelves and placing them in the cart!

I did have a frightening experience with the both of them when Candice was five and Jesse was three years old. We went to the zoo with a neighbor, and her five-year-old daughter. The zoo was small but there was an enclosed pavilion. That particular day it was very crowded because local students were having a field trip. I had Jesse in a stroller to be able to keep an eye on him, but Candice was walking by my side along with my neighbor holding onto her daughter's hand. We were all packed in the pavilion like sardines. Everyone was being shoved to move forward while looking at the monkeys and seals. When I looked down to make sure Candice was next to me, she was gone! Her little friend was still walking next to us. I panicked and started to yell out her name! It seemed like an eternity before I was able to push through the crowd to get to the other end of the pavilion. I saw Candice with tears streaming down her face holding onto a woman's hand, waiting for me to find her. She asked Candice, "Is that your mommy?" I ran to her pushing the stroller and hugged her tightly while trying to catch my breath. I was so grateful to the woman who found her and kept her safe. We went home shortly after the incident, and I was still trembling. I knew at that point that I needed to make sure I had another set of eyes when venturing out with them while they were young.

As they grew, I continued to think of ways to keep them safe. They filled our lives with so much joy and love that I could never imagine my life without them. We became very involved in their activities throughout their school years. My husband drove them everywhere, and I was always with them. We watched them participate in soccer, martial arts, tennis, and harp lessons until they both graduated from high school.

During one of Jesse's middle school soccer games, his game of choice, I had what we would call a *retinitis pigmentosa* (RP) moment. Watching the game and following the soccer ball and my son was challenging for me with my narrowing visual field. He played forward, which meant he would run with the ball down the field to try to score a goal. At this one particular game, the score was tied. I was comfortably sitting in a lawn chair on the sidelines along with the rest of the parents of the team. I looked across the field and was searching for his number on the jerseys. I was certain that Jesse had the ball and was driving it down the field for a goal! With excitement, I yelled out like a crazy soccer mom, "Go, Jesse, go!" Then a few seconds later I heard a soft voice, "Mom, I'm right here next to you." All the parents on the sidelines joined in on our laughter!

The series of RP moments increased as I lost more visual field. I can remember going to a shoe store with my husband and son looking for winter boots. I did not realize that my husband and son had walked away to wait for me while I browsed for boots. Another customer and her friend came up by my left side and proceeded to pick up a pair of boots next to the ones I was looking at. Thinking she was my husband, I said, "I don't like those boots. They are ugly." I looked up and saw my husband and son standing about fifteen feet away, and while I was horrified at my blunder, my husband and son got a real good chuckle out of that RP moment!

Dimly lit and noisy places can give way to RP/Usher moments, and relying on sighted guides does not always keep me out of trouble. On this occasion I was with some family members and friends at a small cabaret in our town. The venue seated approximately 100 people and had long, banquet-style tables with chairs lined along the tables. It was very dimly lit, and my daughter was guiding me to find our table and seat. Other family members were already seated and witnessed what was about to happen. I was guided through a very narrow path, walking in front of people who were already seated.

My daughter stopped, and I interpreted that as a cue to sit down. I stood in front of what I thought was an empty chair and proceeded to bend down while grabbing the seat of the chair. A man was sitting in this chair, and I groped his thighs all the way to his hips to get my bearings! At this point my family broke into laughter, and I realized what I had done. I quickly turned to the fellow sitting in the chair and apologized profusely while trying to contain my laughter. My niece had been instructing me not to sit down, but I couldn't hear her! The gentleman was such a good sport that his comment was, "I haven't had this great of a time in a long time!" And my daughter's comment to him was, "She doesn't get out very often!"

RESTAURANTS AND DRIVING

Restaurant buffet lines can be a very tricky area for individuals with RP and Usher syndrome. One day, my family and I were at the Holiday Inn in Boston, and they had a very nice continental spread for breakfast. My sister-in-law guided me to the line and was in front of me as we put food on our plates, while my son was behind me; at least I thought he was. I wanted more eggs on my plate and stepped to my right and asked a man who I thought was my son, "Can you put more eggs on my plate?" He did without question or comment, but when I went back to our table I realized I had asked a stranger because Jesse was already seated at the table! That poor man probably thought I was bossy!

Not being able to drive has not kept me from doing things or going places. I learned to adapt, but I still missed being behind the wheel. To fill the void of not driving I decided to mow our lawn with our tractor rider lawn mower. What was I thinking? We have a large, somewhat wooded backyard. I memorized where every tree, rock, and creek were located on our property. Our backyard would become very wet after a lot of rain, and I could not tell if the grass was wet unless I walked on it. That, however, did not stop me from mowing the area. You guessed it! I put the rider mower deep in the mud up to its axel, not once but six times!

There was a tree log embedded in a hole as a landmark in the backyard, and one time I missed it and ran over it. I heard a funny grind, but I ignored it and then realized the blades were not turning. I decided it was time to quit and bring the mower up front for my husband to take a look at it. When I drove it up to the front yard and backed it up to turn, the log that measured a foot long became dislodged from under the mower deck! I did not tell my husband that story! It became my little secret. I had to be crazy to even attempt to mow the lawn with our rider, with limited vision, but I wanted to be able to have control of "driving."

I always tell people that having Usher syndrome allowed us to always be together as a family. It was always the four of us. Both of my children are adults now and on their own, but we miss going to all their extracurricular activities and being an active part of their lives.

Now at age 60, I still have some functional central vision left and continue to do everything around the house, and I am very involved in family functions. When I look back, I ask myself, "Why was I so afraid of raising my children? Why did I allow my fears to consume me?" It was the unknown, the uncertainty, in part because so little was known about Usher syndrome. Over the years I have had to adapt to changes in vision, hearing, and find ways to do things safely. However, as the retina specialist told the director of the Korean adoption agency, I was able to raise them and keep them safe with what vision I had.

ABOUT THE AUTHOR

Anna Marie Sengillo was born in Italy and came to the US with her family as a small child. She was diagnosed with moderate hearing loss at the age of 8 and with Usher syndrome in 1981 at the age of 26. Clinically, it is believed to be Usher syndrome type 2A.

Ms. Sengillo graduated from Rochester Institute of Technology in 1977 with a B.A. in Applied Science as a licensed Nuclear Medicine Technologist. She changed careers and was employed by Eastman Kodak Company for 8 years as a research technologist in film before retiring to raise her two children at the age of 32. She loves working around her home and has become the family and friends' computer troubleshooting consultant. Anna enjoys creating DVD slideshows for her family and friends. Her community service includes organizing and raising funds for the Western New York FFB (Foundation Fighting Blindness) VisionWalk. Anna currently resides in New York with her husband and continues to enjoy her family, friends, and the RP/Usher community.

CHAPTER 6

LIFE WITH A MOM WHO HAS USHER SYNDROME

ANNA SENGILLO'S TWO CHILDREN SHARE THEIR STORIES, BOTH HUMOROUS AND COMPASSIONATE, ABOUT LIFE WITH THEIR USHER MOTHER.

JESSE & CANDICE SENGILLO

Admittedly, we found it difficult to plan writing this piece around a central theme, but we know why we struggled to unravel a profound thought, a unique insight, or present an inspiring conclusion. This is because growing up with our mom, who has Usher syndrome type 2, was probably not much different than growing up with a non-affected mother. Our mom never shared her burden or let her disease hinder her role as a mother. She played with us, taught us how to read, came to every sports game, and went the extra mile and more to help us. Although she didn't drive because of *retinitis pigmentosa*, she found a way to take us places. She was and is the best mom we could ever imagine. Our mom just happened to have Usher syndrome.

Jesse: It is easier for us to comment as "grown-ups" who have a mother with Usher syndrome. As my sister and I grew older, especially around our early teen years, we asked more about our mom's condition. Having a loved one who is visually and hearing impaired gives you a closer look at the challenges they experience on a daily basis. For example, needing more light for daily tasks, seeking reading materials with a nice size font, or avoiding injury from bumping into objects. I bet others with a visually and hearing impaired parent can relate to the feeling you get when a stranger responds rudely after having been bumped into by your parent—the desire to provide them an explanation of your parent's condition in a way that makes them regret their response. I also noticed I have adopted various opinions from my mom. For example, I cannot stand it when restaurants are poorly lit or when electronic devices have limited visual/auditory accessibility. Regardless of how reasonable or unreasonable my views are, they simply exist in me as a way of hoping my mom is comfortable on a daily basis.

When you have a loved one with Usher syndrome, you never truly stop worrying about them. It is common to have an uneasy feeling in your stomach as you drop off your parent at a store or feel your heart start racing if they accidentally bump into something at home. Opthalmologist appointments can be trying during the time that you are waiting for the physician to hopefully say "things are stable" with a smile.

However, along with the struggles, there are many times when her condition has provided us all with stories we can laugh about together. Once at a soccer game, my mom was cheering me on as a player dribbled the ball and then turned left and laughed with my friends and me when she saw me next to her. Our favorite story is when she flipped two light switches, one of which was powering my dad's CPAP facemask (a mask providing continuous positive airway pressure, used by people with sleep apnea) while he tried to sleep. This caused it to form a vacuum around his mouth, to which he started laughing and mumbling through the vacuum, "Turn on the switch!" His mumbling was inaudible, as my mom didn't have her hearing aids on, so she turned the two switches off, which turned the lights back off and restarted the face mask. Now that he could talk, he tried to explain what had just happened, but because he had started talking my mom flipped both switches again in an effort to see and hear him better. The facemask became a vacuum again and the whole process repeated.

Candice: My mom's condition has also provided for a number of stories outside of the family. One night, a number of us went out to watch an off-Broadway show. It was my mom, a few cousins, aunts, and myself. Because of our number, we took up almost an entire row. My mom had reached what she thought was an empty seat, and bent over to sit, putting her hand on what she thought was the chair, so she could guide herself. However, a man was occupying this seat and in the end he had a big smile on his face. He told my mom, after she realized she had inadvertently groped his thigh and apologized, that it was the best time he'd had in a while. Everyone including my mom began to laugh. Dealing with Usher syndrome seems to almost require that one has a sense of humor and be able to laugh about incidents like this one.

Our mom has adapted to her eyesight changes and, amazingly, at times is even better than we are finding lost items or figuring out where we all need to go. Whenever I lose something, even to this day with a narrow visual field, she's usually the one who will find it. I'll have searched all over, and within minutes after asking my mom, she'll be the one to spot it first. It's almost like having a narrow visual field makes it easier for her to focus on a specific area. She's usually the one who is on top of everything, with the rest of us oftentimes depending on her.

Jesse: The thing that I admire most about my mom is her dedication to our family. For over five years she took care of her ailing father, my grandfather, three times a day. She woke him up every morning, ensuring he was starting his day with no issues. She gave him his medications and prepared his food. Most importantly, she had a significant role in keeping him calm and comfortable. Seven years after the passing of our grandpa, my mom assumed the caretaking role again with her mother-in-law, my grandma on my dad's side. While other family members were at work, she would catch a ride over to our grandma's house in the morning and take care of her just like she had her own father. The course of our grandma's illness was faster, requiring more medical attention, yet our grandma felt safest when our mom was there. Every time a doctor or healthcare professional made recommendations or a plan of care, grandma would look to our mom for approval. I will never forget the numerous times our grandma would lean back, take a deep breath, and say, "I do not know what we would do without her." It was at these moments when we realized our mom was a great example of how a child should care for his or her parents. I look back on situations like this one and think about how difficult it must be to take care of a parent, and yet with limited eyesight and severe hearing loss, my mom never missed a beat or complained.

Candice: Not only has she stepped up to the plate with other family members, but having grown up with her, I can't imagine how she could have been a better mom. She was always there for us when we were little, caring for my brother and me every day. As we grew older, she was always at every event we had, whether it was for sports, theater, etc. As adults we know that's still the same, and if we ever need her, she'll be right there for us. Our experience growing up with a parent with Usher syndrome was having an incredible mom whom we couldn't love more.

ABOUT THE AUTHORS

Jesse Sengillo is a native of New York. He graduated with a B.S. in Biochemistry from the University of Rochester. Currently, he is a third year medical student in Brooklyn, New York, pursuing Ophthalmology with the hopes of some day helping patients like his mother. He enjoys soccer, tennis, and rooting for the Buffalo Bills in his spare time. Jesse is an active and proud member of the FFB (Foundation Fighting Blindness) with his mother and has participated in the New York City and Los Angeles Vision-Walks.

Candice Sengillo was born in Korea, was adopted as a baby, and has lived in Rochester, New York, since then. She is a graduate of Case Western Reserve University School of Law in Ohio. Currently, she is an assistant District Attorney for Monroe County in Rochester, New York. She enjoys playing tennis and reading. Candice is also a professional harpist and enjoys playing for weddings and special events.

CHAPTER 7

MY LIFE ADJUSTMENTS WITH USHER

FROM A DIAGNOSIS OF DEAFNESS AT AGE 2 TO IMPENDING
BLINDNESS AS A SINGLE MOTHER WITH BOTH USHER
SYNDROME AND COATS DISEASE AT 23, JENNI TRAINS FOR A
NEW CAREER AND REFUSES TO GIVE UP. THIS IS A STORY WITH A
VERY HAPPY ENDING.

JENNI THOMPSON

When my parents first found out that I was hearing impaired, they were not able to find out what caused the hearing loss and were told that I would never speak or grow up in the hearing world. I was placed in a school for the deafblind at the age of two where I learned ASL (American Sign Language) and got speech therapy. My parents, however, never gave up, and they bought me hearing aids hoping they would help. I did extremely well with them and learned to speak without a problem. By the age of six, I was able to attend public school, was mainstreamed, and grew up in the hearing world.

I was twenty, married, and pregnant with my first child when I started experiencing more hearing and vision problems. The doctor wanted to do an MRI to make sure there were no tumors in the brain, but they couldn't because of the pregnancy. Instead, I went to the ophthalmologist for what I thought would be a routine eye exam to get a new prescription for contacts. It was then that the doctor said there was something wrong with my eyes and I needed to go see a retina specialist.

I saw the specialist, and he told me that I had *retinitis pigmentosa*, but I honestly don't remember my reaction. I had not noticed any problems with my visual field, but the doctor said that he thought that I would go completely blind by age of thirty. For me that seemed forever away, and I thought that I would deal with it someday.

As I continued living my life, the doctor's words were always in the back of my mind, but I did little to prepare until I was twenty-three years old. At that time I went through a horrible divorce and had two little children. I had no work experience or college education. I was trying to work to take care of my kids, but minimum wage was not paying the bills or giving us the life I wanted for my family.

I reached out to Vocational Rehabilitation for the Blind hoping they could help me find a job. There I heard about the Lions World Services for the Blind, a program designed to teach living skills, as well as job training. At first I refused to listen because my home was in Utah, and I would have had to go to Little Rock, Arkansas, and that, in turn, would require me to leave my children in the care of someone else for six months. I told my VR (Vocational Rehabilitation) counselor there was no way I would do that!

After several months of searching for a job that would pay more and work with my disability, I was not having any luck. My VR counselor approached me again about Lions World, and that time I listened. I knew that this was something I had to do. She continued to explain that it was a program that had a contract with the IRS (Internal Revenue Service) to hire people with a visual impairment or who were blind, and they guaranteed a job with them. I didn't know how I was going to do it or survive being away from my kids for that long, but I knew I had to do it. I spoke with my family, who were very supportive about my decision. We were able to make arrangements for my children, and I left to go to Lions World. By then I was twenty-five years old, and this was the hardest thing I had done in my life, but it was also the best thing I had ever done.

Once I completed the program, I came back with an excellent job with benefits. The IRS was great working with me and my disability, providing all the accessibility technology I needed. I worked for the IRS for nine years and worked my way up the career ladder there, eventually becoming a Revenue Officer. This position allowed me to work from home, but I had to go in the office once a week and go out in the field once a week. Over time it became difficult to do my job, and I had to stop working at the IRS because I developed another eye disease called Coats disease, which is taking my central vision.

USHER + COATS = MORE ADJUSTMENTS

I have noticed that as I lose more vision, my hearing has gotten worse because I can no longer see people's faces, and that keeps me from being able to read their lips. I was not only struggling with work, but with my everyday life, so I decided it would be best to retire. I feel that I need to focus on getting training for myself so that I can remain independent and live as much of a normal life as possible. Of course, it is not a definite retirement because I hope to be able to get training in natural healing, especially foot zone therapy, a massage used to treat different body ailments. This job would be great for me as a deafblind person because I could work from home, set my own schedule, and be one-on-one with the clients, enabling me to hear them better. No phones! And I could use my hands to feel what I am doing, so I would not need my eyes.

My hearing loss is in the profound range now. I have decided to get a cochlear implant and will be getting this done in a few months. I am feeling all the emotions one can possibly think of at the moment: nervous, scared, excited, and hopeful. I hope that I can improve my hearing so that I can continue to interact with the world, my family and friends.

Right now I may not know the direction I am going, but I know God is watching over me and guiding me through my life. There have been times when I wanted to give up and sit at home and do nothing and feel sorry for myself, but my husband and kids keep me going. To better prepare for what may be ahead, I am currently attending school at the Division Services for the Blind and Visually Impaired, where I am learning basic living skills as a blind person, Including how to cook, use the computer, clean, and develop braille and cane travel skills. I am also taking a woodshop class there and learning to use regular power tools to make wooden bowls and a cutting board. By preparing myself, I hope that someday I will be able to help others see through their trials.

For the longest time I felt alone, and it seemed like no one understood what I was going through, until just recently, when I met a group of ladies with Usher syndrome. They keep me going. We are able to laugh and enjoy life, as well as share our struggles. We are all at different stages in our lives, but we can understand each other. If we put our trust in God and try to be as active in our community as possible, I know anything is possible.

Being a deafblind person is not easy, and sometimes it is challenging, but we are human, we want to be treated as equals, and we strive to be successful. Being able to hear other Usher stories is also something that keeps me going. I know there are others out there who feel and struggle as I do, but we keep our heads up and smile while we keep one foot in front of the other and accomplish whatever we want in life. There are times we want to give up and feel it is impossible to go on, but I want to show the world that I can do this. It is important to be a good role model, and I will not let Usher syndrome stop me.

ABOUT THE AUTHOR

Jenni Thompson was born and raised in northern Utah, where she currently resides with her two beautiful children and her husband. She was diagnosed with hearing loss at 18 months old, diagnosed with *retinitis pigmentosa* at age 20, and later received genetic confirmation of Usher syndrome type 2A.

She is presently in the process of retiring from her position with the IRS. She is certified in foot zone therapy and hopes to continue her studies in natural healing, nutrition and aromatherapy. She loves to help people and would like to help others overcome their health issues, trials, and tribulations.

This story is dedicated to her family and friends who have loved and supported her throughout her life. To her mother, an amazing woman, who taught her how to be strong. To her children, the love of her life, who were forced to grow up faster than most kids their age. And to her husband, who chose to marry her knowing that she had Usher syndrome.

Chapter 8

A CHILD'S POINT OF VIEW

As her mother loses more sight and hearing, Jenni Thompson's 15-year-old daughter finds inspiration and a role model on being strong ... even though she, too, could have a child with Usher syndrome in later life.

CHEYENNE THOMPSON

Ever since I was little, I knew that my mom had a disease that would eventually make her go deaf and blind. I knew it would happen someday, but it never really hit me until July of 2014. I was 14 years old. We were on a family trip to Lake Powell, Utah, and my mom's eyes were not doing very well. It was late at night, and we were walking around the houseboat. I was guiding my mom around because she was unable to see in the dark. I looked over at her blank face and her empty eyes, and that was when it hit me: My mom is going blind. She will not be able to look at me on my wedding day. She isn't going to know what my children, her grandchildren, look like. These thoughts still haunt me.

After July had passed, reality seemed to hit me like a ton of bricks. Mom gave up driving in September, and when I turned fifteen in December, I immediately began driving everywhere for her. When I found out that my mom would be retiring early from her job due to her failing eyesight and hearing, it seemed to hit me all over again. When I was younger, I refused to think about my mom going blind. I thought that if I didn't think about it, then it wouldn't come true. Now it had become real life.

Along with the narrowing tunnel vision, she was also going deaf. She lost the ability to lip read because of her failing eyesight, and that interfered with the ability to understand speech with her limited hearing. In the spring of 2015, she qualified to receive a cochlear implant. This technology would be surgically implanted in the ear and could help the patient hear sounds and speech again.

My mom had the surgery in June of that year and was told that it could take up to a year for the cochlear to begin to work. At first everything just sounded like ringing and beeping to her. Four months later, she was able to make out certain sounds and noises. Her brain had to re-learn how to interpret what she heard because hearing through the cochlear is something completely new. As time passes, she is becoming more and more able to hear everyday noises that we normal hearing people don't even realize we can hear. She still has a long road ahead of her before she can follow conversation using this new technology, but I'm grateful that it can help her communicate, especially as she loses more sight.

As the progression of my mother's condition has become a reality and I have matured, some new fears have made their way into my head. The disease that my mom had been diagnosed with, Usher syndrome type 2A, is genetic and I am an automatic carrier. That means that if I have children with someone who is a carrier of the same gene, then there is a one in four chance that my child will have it. The possibility of having a child with Usher syndrome would make some people decide not to have children at all. I know I want to have children, but I'm still scared. Watching my mom go through life with Usher syndrome has been hard on me because I feel helpless not knowing how I can help her. I don't know if I would be able to go through it all over again. I haven't allowed myself to think about this situation much because the unknown can often be terrifying. It's hard to face the reality of something that I thought was way off into the future.

Watching my mom go through so many challenges, watching her struggling to see and hear, has been one of the hardest yet most inspiring experiences of my life. I know that if she can overcome these challenges, I will be able to overcome any challenges I encounter in my life.

Before she found the "Usher Chicks," a group of local women who have Usher syndrome, I could tell she was having a hard time, physically and emotionally, and that she felt alone. I wanted to help her so badly but I didn't understand what she was going through. No matter what I did, I still couldn't understand what she was going through and neither could anyone else in my family. Once she found the Usher Chicks, things began to change. She seemed so much happier. It did her good to have people who understood the kind of things that she was dealing with, and I'm so glad she found them. They are now a big part of her support system.

I had the opportunity to go to the 2015 RP (*retinitis pigmentosa*) Social with my mom. At this event for people with RP and Usher syndrome, I met many people that my mom had become friends with online or in person. We took them sightseeing and went to a museum and to lunch. To me, it was comforting to meet these people and see how independent they are able to be. It helps me to know that with a little time and a little practice, my mom will still be able to have some of the freedoms that she wants.

I know that life with Usher has been tough for my mom, and I'm so proud of how strong and determined to succeed she is. She could have completely given up. She could have decided to just sit at home and do nothing. I know that's probably what I would have done. But instead, she prepared herself professionally and worked hard to be able to provide for our family in any way she could. It could not have been easy for her to go to school to learn to do everything as a blind person for two months. I know it was very difficult for me not having her there with me all the time, but I can't imagine what it was like for her.

My mom inspires me everyday to be strong and to never give up. No matter how difficult one's circumstances are, there is always a way to turn it around and make it a positive experience. I'm grateful for her strength and willingness to move forward. She has been so brave facing all the challenges, and she is truly the most inspiring person in my life. She is my hero.

I'm also so grateful for the support that has been given to my family. Everyone has been so caring and so willing to help us in any way he or she can. It has shown me how truly amazing friends, family, and complete strangers can be. So many kind souls have helped my family in more ways than anyone will ever know, and we can't thank them all enough. Yet, every single one is truly a blessing from God.

ABOUT THE AUTHOR

Cheyenne Thompson is the daughter of Jenni Thompson. She wrote this when she was 15 years old and a sophomore in high school. She is currently on her high school drill team, and she has been dancing for twelve years. She hopes to graduate and go to college to become a registered nurse. She loves her family very much, especially her mother who is also her best friend.

CHAPTER 9

SCALING MOUNTAINS

THE MOTHER OF TWO USH1F GIRLS TALKS ABOUT EXPLORING COMMUNICATION ALTERNATIVES... AND MAKING HISTORY.

MELISSA CHAIKOF

THE BEGINNING

Before I had children, I worked full time at an engineering consulting company. When I was near the end of my pregnancy with my first child, my supervisor asked me to interview a prospective candidate for a job in our department. The man I interviewed was profoundly deaf and communicated orally, using his hearing aid and lip reading. At the time, I knew nothing about deafness or deaf education, but he impressed me greatly.

Rachel was born about a month later, on May 7, 1987, and my parents flew to Boston from their home in Baltimore to see the baby and help my husband Elliot and me during the first week. I don't know exactly when or what first made me suspect a problem with Rachel's hearing, but my first conscious memory of thinking about it was when I took my mother to the airport and she told me not to slam the door because I would wake the baby. I know that I was already aware then, because I remember thinking that I wasn't so sure it would wake her. At some point during Rachel's first week of life, I had already noticed that she didn't startle to loud sounds.

My husband was then a surgical resident, and he looked up babies and hearing in one of his medical school textbooks. He found something saying that babies don't respond normally to sound until the age of four months, and we both latched onto that. However, we continued to grow uneasy. When I said something to our pediatrician at Rachel's first visit when she was about three weeks old, he told me I was "an overly anxious new mother who didn't understand how newborns react to sound." At her two-month checkup, he noticed her head control was poor, something I wasn't aware of because Rachel was my first child. She would bob her head up and down on my shoulder because her neck muscles were weak. He suspected cerebral palsy and referred us to a pediatric neurologist. The neurologist did all sorts of tests but did not mention Rachel's hearing until I asked him about it. He then did a few rudimentary tests and said that we could have her tested.

The night before Rachel's hearing test, the smoke alarm went off in the hall right outside her room when I burned something cooking. She was happily playing in her crib and didn't even flinch as the alarm was blaring. I knew it wasn't good. The next day, we took her to Massachusetts Eye and Ear for an ABR (*auditory brainstem response*) test. It was only supposed to take about an hour, but we waited for 2½ hours in the waiting room knowing as time went on that we weren't going to get good news. When the audiologist brought us back into the room, she told us Rachel had a severe-to-profound hearing loss. That terminology meant nothing to me at the time, and so I asked her if Rachel was deaf.

The audiologist immediately took us to meet with another audiologist and a social worker. Elliot and I were in shock and were not thinking straight. The audiologist and social worker proceeded to ask us if we knew anything about the controversy in deaf education. When we told her no, she told us that there were those who believed in sign language, those who supported an oral approach, and those who believed in using both. I don't remember their exact words, but they pushed the Total Communication (TC) approach in their presentation. Knowing nothing, we replied that we guessed both would be good. They then gave us one referral, to a TC school, and sent us off.

TRYING TO FIND OUR WAY

I spent the first 24 hours after receiving the definitive diagnosis of Rachel's deafness crying. We knew nothing of deafness. We wondered about whether Rachel would have to attend a special school, whether she'd ever be able to speak, where she'd find friends, and we thought about all the joys that hearing brought to our lives that we took for granted and were sad for what she'd be missing.

Then, I made the first connection that helped me immeasurably. My father was the lower school principal at a private school in Baltimore. Unbeknownst to me, he had a deaf student in his school. He put me in contact with the girl's mother, Esther, and she told me about the oral approach and about the A.G. Bell Association for the Deaf. When we went to Baltimore to visit my parents a few weeks later, she had us over to her house along with a friend of hers who also had a daughter who was deaf and oral. She had reams of information ready for me, and having someone guide me through the early stages of learning about deafness was both invaluable and comforting.

Even though we were convinced by speaking to Esther that we were on the right track with the oral approach, we still explored all of our options. We contacted the Massachusetts Association for the Deaf and received names of a few families in the area who were using the various approaches. We spoke at length with two families– one that was oral, whose ten-year-old son was doing beautifully and could even carry on a conversation while riding his bike, and one whose daughter had had meningitis at age three so had had speech and language already. However, the family decided that hearing aids were a pain, got rid of them, and committed to using American Sign Language (ASL). Their daughter was now eight and had lost all of her spoken language. We knew then that we wanted Rachel to have the ease of communication the boy did.

This was in the pre-internet days and information wasn't as readily available as it is for parents today. Instead, I went to the library and copied reams of articles on deaf children and language, many of which I still have in my file today. I also discov-

ered the A.G. Bell Association's book catalog and started order-
ing and reading books that still line my shelf today, books by
Daniel Ling and Arthur Boothroyd and my early "bible," *Learning to Listen*. Later, I added books by Warren Estabrooks. We also
contacted the John Tracy Clinic and began their correspondence
course.

When Rachel was three months old, she received her first
hearing aid. The button attached to an ear mold that stuck out of
her ear. At four months old, she got one for her other ear. I sewed
pockets into "onesie" (one-piece) t-shirts to hold them. The difficult part, though, was that the microphone was on the box, so
keeping the aids under her clothes was not a good idea because
the sound would then become muffled.

When Rachel was four months old, we started out at a program that was overseen by a professor at a graduate school of
Communication Disorders. What benefitted me the most in that
program was a weekly parent group the professor had set up.
Being able to share my feelings with other parents who understood how I was feeling was invaluable in helping me get past
the grieving process and on to focusing all of my efforts on helping Rachel. Unfortunately, the part of the program that was for
Rachel was not overly beneficial.

When Rachel was five months old, I returned to work part-
time. I remembered Ralph, the oral deaf man whom I'd interviewed for a job in my department. I looked him up in the company directory and saw that he was now working in another
department He remembered me and was very surprised to learn
I'd had a deaf baby. He told me all about the Clarke School in
Northampton, Massachusetts, and how happy he had been there.
A few weeks later, he came to my office and asked me to join him
during lunch for a disability fair taking place at our company. He
took me to a table where a teenage girl was with her mother. The
girl was deaf and had gone for five years to Clarke. I spoke with
her and her mother at length and left very encouraged.

Elliot and I drove two hours to Northampton and visited the
Clarke School with Rachel when she was six months old. While
we were impressed with the facilities and with the professionals

there, we left discouraged by the students. At that time, Clarke specialized in very profoundly to totally deaf children. They were all tethered to a center bank by FM cables, and most had very poor speech. In addition, we sat in on a class of 15-year-olds and were very discouraged by the low academic level. This was not the future we wanted for Rachel. We wanted her to be able to hear and speak so that she could communicate with the entire world and not just a small portion, but, at the same time, we didn't want her to struggle so greatly to communicate.

When Rachel was ten months old, she got her first pair of ear level hearing aids. At the same appointment, we learned that Rachel had more hearing than we'd initially thought. Unfortunately, unbeknownst to us at the time, Rachel began to gradually lose her residual hearing right after this appointment. We noticed her diminishing response to sound but thought that it might be because she was experiencing recurring middle ear infections. The ENT (ear-nose-throat) specialist agreed and put tubes in her ears. The ear infections stopped, but her hearing did not improve.

We decided that we needed to find a better program for Rachel and, as I was speaking to Esther on the phone, she said, "If I had to do it all over again, I'd go the Beebe Center." She added that she had met children at an A.G. Bell convention who were learning language through the Auditory-Verbal approach and that she was incredibly impressed by them. I contacted the Beebe Center in Easton, Pennsylvania. At the time, their program was for families from out of town to come learn about the Auditory-Verbal approach and immerse themselves in it for a week. This was in 1988, and there were very few Auditory-Verbal therapists and centers. Rachel had an hour of formal therapy every morning, including with Helen Beebe herself. During the rest of the day, we would watch other families' therapy sessions, speak with other parents, and watch informative videos. One of their therapists visited us during three evenings and showed us how we could incorporate language learning into our everyday lives. For example, she demonstrated how to stand Rachel up on a step ladder and have her help me wash dishes, all the while feeding in language about washing and soap bubbles and hot and cold, wet and dry, etc. After that week was over, we returned home eager to start working with Rachel and also began working with Lea Watson at the Auditory-Verbal Communication Center in Gloucester, Massachusetts, a 54-mile drive each way, for an hour twice a week. I was so committed to the Auditory-Verbal approach after seeing how well the kids were doing with it that I was willing to do whatever it took.

One of the early activities involved using toy animals and vehicles to teach Rachel the "learning to listen sounds." These sounds comprise the full range of speech frequencies, and, if Rachel could learn to discriminate those, then she could learn to discriminate speech. One of those sounds was, "ahhh," which we said while flying a toy airplane. I remember how excited I was the day Rachel picked up the airplane and said, "Ahhh." However, when Rachel was 18 months old, one day she picked up the airplane and mouthed "ahhh" with no voice.

It was around this time that Lea was having difficulty getting Rachel to demonstrate any consistent response to sound or any indication that she was comprehending any spoken language through her hearing. She referred us to one of the only Auditory-Verbal audiologists in the country at the time, Judith Marlowe, in Winter Park, Florida, to see if new ear molds that resulted in a 10+ decibel gain in hearing in others would help Rachel. We had three days booked with Dr. Marlowe. However, after the first day, she told us that Rachel appeared to have absolutely no residual hearing and that there was nothing she could do to help her hear more. She gave us literature on a vibrotactile aid and on the cochlear implant.

Although we did not have much money then, we decided that we needed to try that vibrotactile aid, and so $1000 later, Rachel was wearing a box with two wires that ended with disks that we taped each day to her chest. One vibrated for low frequency sounds and the other for high frequency sounds. The vibrotactile aid proved to be totally useless.

After returning from Florida, we spoke with Lea. Her first reaction was that we needed to find another approach to use with Rachel, that she clearly could not be Auditory-Verbal without the auditory part. However, Lea was reluctant to let us go because we were one of the most Auditory-Verbal families she knew, even though Rachel couldn't hear. She decided she would use the same types of activities she did with her other students but would incorporate lip reading and other visual and tactile cues into her lessons.

We started holding everything we talked about up to our mouths. Rachel proved to have a gift for lip reading, and she very quickly developed a receptive vocabulary list of 100 words. She would also vocalize a few words, although most she still mouthed. We were beginning to get discouraged and were beginning to think we'd have to add some sign language. Then Lea made a connection for us that would change Rachel's and our lives.

COCHLEAR IMPLANTS

Lea was a very active member of Auditory-Verbal International (AVI). One day, she was speaking on the phone with another AVI board member, Judy Simser, in Ottawa. Lea mentioned that she was working with a child who was totally deaf. Judy told Lea that she, too, had a child who was totally deaf, and the family had gone to New York to the cochlear implant center at New York University (NYU) and gotten her a cochlear implant. By this time, it was no longer a single channel cochlear implant but, instead, was the Nucleus 22, the first multichannel cochlear implant. Lea shared this information with us in August of 1989. In October, we spent three days in New York where Rachel was evaluated by the audiologists and therapists at the League for the Hard of Hearing as well as by a child psychologist.

The therapist at the League introduced us to a mother and her daughter, Caitlin, who was hearing and speaking as well as any four year old. We were beyond amazed and knew this was without a doubt what we wanted for Rachel. Two years later, Caitlin and her mom appeared on CBS-TV's *60 Minutes* and showed the world the potential of the cochlear implant for children. Cochlear implants were still in phase III clinical trials for children, and so Caitlin was the only child I knew who followed a similar path to Rachel with spoken language and full mainstreaming. Caitlin has inspired us through the years and showed us what was possible, from playing the piano to attending a top university.

At the end of our three days at NYU, Bill Shapiro, the head audiologist, told us that Rachel was definitely a candidate for a cochlear implant. The FDA strict protocol required that Rachel spend the next eight weeks using a body worn FM hearing aid at all times. If, at the end of the eight weeks, she still showed no response to sound, then she would be a candidate. Eight weeks later, we returned to NYU and, as suspected, Rachel still couldn't hear anything, even with the powerful FM hearing aid. That evening, we checked Rachel into the hospital. In spite of a widespread power outage that would delay the surgery by five hours, Rachel received her cochlear implant. The surgeon was able to insert all the electrodes and pronounced the surgery a success. Three weeks later, we were back in New York for the activation of Rachel's implant. We had no idea what to expect because there were few children with cochlear implants and all we were told was that Rachel would hear environmental sounds. When the audiologist started stimulating the first electrode and reached the point where Rachel could hear the signal, she started to cry. Her crying meant that she could hear! She proceeded to react the same way to each additional electrode.

We were warned that it would take awhile for Rachel's brain to learn to make sense of the sound from the CI (cochlear implant). After two weeks, right before we were supposed to return to New York for Rachel's second mapping, she began to respond to loud sounds by turning her head to look for them. Her tolerance for sound had greatly increased, and Bill was able to give her considerably more power, which meant considerably more hearing. Within a week of her second mapping, Rachel began to respond consistently to voices. We were then able to return to Auditory-Verbal therapy with Lea, this time with hearing. Rachel transitioned from lip-reading to having fully auditory language within six months of receiving her CI. In addition, two months after beginning to hear, Rachel began to use her voice.

MOVING ON

In June of 1991, we moved to Atlanta, Georgia, where my husband would do a fellowship. At this point, we had two children. Our son Adam, who was born with normal hearing, was five months old then. We began working with Mary Ann Costin at the Auditory-Verbal Center in Atlanta, then known as the Auditory Education Center (AEC). Mary Ann evaluated Rachel and identified the areas of language we needed to focus on next. Rather than daycare, Rachel attended a regular preschool five mornings a week, leaving my mornings free to focus on Adam and my afternoons free while he napped to focus on working with Rachel. During that year, I saw how greatly Rachel's language thrived from having me have so much more time to spend with her. Her language, while progressing steadily, was still delayed by about two years, which made sense, since she had not heard anything until she was two years eight months old.

We opted to keep Rachel in preschool an extra year to give her more time to close her language gap. When she entered kindergarten in 1993, she was fully mainstreamed with no special education and did very well, including socially, making friends very quickly. She continued to go to therapy once a week through second grade, and then in third grade we dropped to once a month. At the end of third grade, she "graduated" from Auditory-Verbal therapy.

REPEAT

While newborn hearing screening was not yet routine in 1995 when our third child, Jessica, was born, we were able to have her hearing tested before she left the hospital because we had a family history. Jessica was not yet twenty-four hours old when the hospital audiologist told us that she could not get any response to sound from Jessica. The original theory of a world-renowned pediatric neurologist was that a flu-like virus I had had five months into my pregnancy had resulted both in Rachel's deafness and in an "isolated insult to her central nervous system," resulting also in gross motor delays. Instead, the cause had turned out to be genetic, and so, just as Rachel was nearing the end of her Auditory-Verbal therapy, it was time for us to start over again. Unlike Rachel, Jessica never had any residual hearing and hearing aids proved useless.

One thing we knew was that we didn't want to wait until Jessica was two to get her hearing because we knew all too well how many years we had spent working with Rachel to catch up her language. Thus, at fifteen-months-old, Jessica became the youngest pediatric cochlear implant recipient in the U.S. at that time. The early implant proved to be very beneficial for Jessica. We began our weekly sessions with Mary Ann, and Jessica's receptive language progressed very quickly so that, by age three, it was age appropriate. However, she was barely talking. Because we were experienced Auditory-Verbal parents at that point, we knew something was not right. We noticed that while Jessica could spontaneously make certain sounds, she could not produce them voluntarily when we asked her to repeat them. We took her to a pediatric neurologist who diagnosed her with speech apraxia, a condition where the signal from the brain to the mouth gets jumbled so that the mouth cannot figure out how to form the sounds based on what the ear, or in Jessica's case, her CI, is sending to her brain. Mary Ann referred us to an oral motor therapist who specialized in apraxia, Sharon Wexler. Within two months of working with Sharon, Jessica began to talk. Within five months, her expressive language jumped a year. It was as if all of that language had been inside of her waiting to come out. At age six, Jessica "graduated" from Auditory-Verbal therapy with language that tested age level to two years above in all areas.

Like Rachel, Jessica had gross motor delays. Rachel was sitting up at 10 months and Jessica at 11 months. Rachel was walking at 18 months and Jessica was not walking well until she was 2 years 3 months old. Between that and her expressive language delay, we opted to start Jessica in preschool a year late and put her in with a class of children a year younger.

THE REST OF THE STORY–ALMOST

The one downside to high school, or I should actually say two downsides, were Rachel's cochlear implant failures. One morning in the spring of her ninth grade year, she came to us very agitated, saying that she had put on her processor but was only hearing loud, painful clashing sounds. I immediately took out her spare processor, but when she put it on, she burst into tears. It didn't take the audiologist long to confirm that Rachel's internal implant had failed. The surgeon in Atlanta, Wendell Todd, was wonderful and worked Rachel's surgery in for six days later.

Rachel received a Nucleus 24 Contour, which meant a technology upgrade, in March 2003. She had some auditory comprehension immediately, and, with her excellent lip-reading skills, the combination meant that she could function well in most situations, although not on the phone. Her school provided her with a CART* reporter for the duration of the school year, which also helped a great deal. (*The reporter was trained in Computer Access Realtime Translation, a system for realtime transcription of speech used to help deaf or hearing impaired people. The typed text appears almost instantly on a nearby video monitor.)

It took Rachel about ten months to attain a level of auditory comprehension comparable to what she'd had with her Nucleus 22. Unfortunately, she only got to enjoy that for three weeks. One morning, I received a phone call from her school. Rachel was hearing static. I called our audiologist, and we were very fortunate that the Cochlear Corporation audiologist was going to be in Atlanta that day doing integrity testing on a few other children and was able to fit Rachel in at the end. While the integrity testing did not show a problem with Rachel's implant, because Rachel at 16 was an accurate reporter of what she was hearing, Cochlear Corporation told us to go ahead and re-implant. What happened to Rachel had less than a 1% chance of occurring. We were very upset to have Rachel go through yet another surgery, but, at the same time, we were fortunate that Cochlear Corporation was so cooperative. We decided to simultaneously have her original ear re-implanted and her other ear implanted for the first time. After one very long eight-hour day, Rachel had her two new implants.

We were weary at that point of adjusting to a new CI. Once again, even though she went from a Nucleus 24 to another Nucleus 24, Rachel could not hear as well with her new CI. While we did not expect her to hear clearly from her new ear, we did not expect her readjustment to take as long this time. I repeatedly took her back to her audiologist for mappings, but they didn't help. Four months into it, I made the decision to take her up to Bill Shapiro at NYU. That proved to be one of the best decisions we could have made. The difference in Rachel's hearing after those two days was nothing short of incredible. In the booth, her auditory comprehension jumped 20%. In everyday life, that meant the difference between struggling to hear, to using her cell phone with the regular earpiece without the telecoil while walking down the noisy main hallway of her school at the end of the day and not missing a beat.

Over time, Rachel not only attained her previous level of hearing with her Nucleus 22 but, especially with her bilateral implants, she exceeded it. It is comforting knowing that the chances of her ever going completely without hearing again are slim since it's very unlikely that both implants would ever fail at the same time. We also opted to have Jessica bilaterally implanted. Jessica heard incredibly well with her one CI, which was a good thing because, no matter how hard I actually tried to teach her, she could not lip-read at all, not even a single word. We felt she needed a "spare ear" so that she would never be left without hearing. Jessica was nine years old when she received her bilateral CI about two months after Rachel received hers. Within a year, she was hearing as well out of her new ear as her original.

Rachel had always excelled in and loved art. She was accepted early admission to Savannah College of Art and Design (SCAD) and so was able to sit back and enjoy her senior year without the added stress of the college application process.

THE MOUNTAIN

Just as we thought we'd come to the end of our long journey, almost like climbing a very tall hill for nineteen years, and now thought we could sit back and enjoy the view, we found a mountain looming in front of that hill. Both of my girls and I have always worn glasses. Thus, in July 2006, we went together for our annual ophthalmology appointments. We were seeing two new doctors at Emory. When Rachel and I met up in the waiting room waiting for our eyes to dilate, she asked me if anyone had ever said anything before about her having a constricted visual field. I felt my stomach drop but tried to remain outwardly calm for Rachel's sake. Early on, we had learned of a genetic cause of deafness, Usher syndrome. All of those with Usher syndrome type 1 are born profoundly deaf with vestibular issues. However, all those born profoundly deaf with vestibular issues do not have Usher syndrome. Most children with Usher 1 are diagnosed with RP (*retinitis pigmentosa*) by age ten. However, even though the ophthalmologist we had been seeing knew that I was concerned about it, it had gone undetected until Rachel was nineteen. As difficult as it had been nineteen years earlier to get the news of Rachel's deafness, learning that both of my girls had Usher syndrome was far worse. Only Rachel understood it at the time, and watching her crying and trying to cope with the news was the most painful thing I have had to live through. Finding this out a month before she was to start her freshman year at a visual arts college only added to the pain.

Rachel graduated from college, followed by graduate school at University College London, and in the fall of 2014, she realized one of her dreams when she began serving in the Peace Corps in Cameroon, Africa. She is working in the area of health education, focusing in particular on helping those with disabilities. You can read about her experiences on her blog at http://blog.rachel-chaikof.com.

Jessica discovered a love of science while in high school and has just completed her first year at Wheaton College in Massachusetts. She is majoring in chemistry, with plans to continue on to graduate school and then both to teach and do research.

VISION FOR THE FUTURE

Rachel cites her philosophy in the form of a quote, "Today is a gift. That's why it's called the present." That is how she views her RP. We want to ensure that she and Jessica continue to enjoy the gifts and beauty of every day, and, thus, we are determined to work to bring a cure or effective treatment for Usher 1F to fruition.

ABOUT THE AUTHOR

Melissa Chaikof is married to Elliot Chaikof, and they have three children, Rachel, Adam, and Jessica. Rachel and Jessica have Usher syndrome type 1F, the leading cause of deaf-blindness among those who are Jewish. Melissa has a B.A. in applied math from the University of Pennsylvania and an M.S. in mathematical sciences from Johns Hopkins University. She was very active over the years in advocating for cochlear implants and listening and spoken language for children who are deaf. However, since her daughters received the Usher syndrome diagnosis, she changed her focus to working to find a cure for the vision loss of Usher 1F. After working in nonprofit fundraising and development for 12 years, she left her job to focus on Usher 1F Collaborative, Inc., a 501(c)(3) non-profit organization she and Elliot founded in 2013 to fund research for a cure for Usher 1F. For further information, visit http://usher1f.org.

CHAPTER 10

SEARCHING FOR THE LIGHT IN THE DARKNESS

THE YOUNGEST PERSON EVER TO RECEIVE A COCHLEAR IMPLANT WRITES OF HER CHALLENGES FROM GIRL SCOUT CAMP TO COLLEGE CHEMISTRY CLASSES.

JESSICA CHAIKOF

I t was a clear and dark autumn night in 2005 at the Girl Scout Camp, Pine Acres, in Georgia. It was late at night, and the full moon was out. The leaves were beginning to turn, since fall was at its full course. This was my first year as a Girl Scout; therefore, it was the first camping trip that I had ever been on. Earlier that evening, we had had a fantastic time roasting *s'mores* by the fire, telling each other ghost stories, and singing camp songs. It was every normal possible activity that one could think of to do on an average camping trip. Little did I know that those "normal times" would end soon.

I lay wide-awake in my bed too excited to sleep because of what was to come the next day. Suddenly, someone started to nudge my shoulder, and I turned around to see my buddy standing there staring at me with the look saying, "I need to go to the bathroom."

"Now? You already went like two hours ago!" I said with a groan because I did not feel like leaving the cabin again.

"I cannot go by myself. You know the rule. You have to go with your buddy," she responded. Even though I could not hear her because I did not have my cochlear implants turned on, I knew that was exactly what she said to me. The buddy system that our troop leaders had installed was seriously starting to get on my nerves. I flung myself out of bed, grabbed my cochlear implant processor, put my shoes on, and picked up a flashlight. Then I met my buddy at the door, and off we went.

The leaves crunched under our feet as we made our way to the bathroom in pitch-blackness. With full confidence, my buddy ran ahead of me, but I, on the other hand, was too timid to run. Even though my flashlight was on full power and was bright as the sun, I still had trouble seeing. I could not see the building ahead of me or the twigs and branches that lay in our way. Filled with fear of the idea of tripping or bumping into something, with my flashlight shining I walked slowly towards the building. Eventually, I reached the building and decided to use the bathroom while waiting for her.

After she was done using the bathroom, we exited the building. The moment the exit doors opened, the cold night air embraced me. My heart raced with anticipation of getting back to my cabin safely. I grabbed my buddy's hand, and as we took our first step outside, I felt her hand disappear from mine. There I was, standing outside alone in the cold and the dark. Desperate to get back to my cabin, I shined my flashlight towards my buddy. I found her at a cabin and assumed it was our cabin. I got to the cabin and shined my flashlight into it in order to make sure we were at the right one. My buddy just opened the door and entered. The inside of the cabin felt odd and eerily unfamiliar to me. My gut kept telling me it was not the right cabin. I turned around and said to my buddy, "I don't think we are in the right cabin."

One of the girls jumped out of the bed, and said, "What are you guys doing here? It's the middle of the night." Right then I realized that we were indeed in the wrong cabin, and I had just fallen for my buddy's infamous prank because I could not see. My buddy looked at me like it was no big deal, but I felt humiliated. My stomach felt sick, and I had never been so embarrassed in my entire life. How could I have trusted my buddy? I trusted her with my life and dignity. Needless to say, I did not trust my buddy with my safety for a long time or probably ever again.

Several months later I was diagnosed with Usher syndrome at what was a seemly normal doctor's appointment with my sister Rachel. I remember sitting in the room with Rachel, playing Kirby on my Gameboy, paying little attention to what the doctor was saying to her. Until suddenly something caught my attention. My sister was crying in tears nonstop. Rachel had just been diagnosed with Usher syndrome. At the time, I understood little of what was going on, and the fact that my life would also change forever.

As much of a cliché as it sounds, it was true: my life did change. Rachel stopped driving due to her vision, and my parents became hesitant about letting me learn to drive. After months of thinking, my parents decided not to let me get a learner's permit because of my safety. As time went by, my day vision slowly began to worsen, but I was still able to see well. However, my night vision began to quickly deteriorate. At the time, it did not bother me much because I had all of the help I needed. My parents were still able to drive me to places, and everyone always knew to help me at night.

In the beginning of my junior year of high school at my IEP (individualized education program) meeting, everyone started to suggest that I should learn how to use a white cane. Adamantly, I refused because I did not want to be seen as weak or different from my peers. However, in my senior year the idea was brought up again because I was going to college the following year. With an inward groan, I agreed that I would learn to use one, but with the condition that I would not have to use it unless I needed it. In June of 2014, I attended the first of three freshman orientations for Wheaton College in Norton, Massachusetts. My mom suggested that I take my cane in case I needed it, so I decided to put it at the bottom of my suitcase so no one would see it. As we were leaving, we came upon some uneven wooden stairs without a railing. In an instant, my heart thudded in fear against my chest, and I paused in the middle of the stairs. I had no idea what to do about getting help because I was on my own, and I did not know anyone. Plus, I was nervous about asking somebody for help. Eventually, somebody saw what was happening and offered to help. At that moment, I knew that the secret was out because what was the point of keeping it if I could not be safe?

Currently, I am a rising sophomore at Wheaton College, with hopes of majoring in chemistry. In more ways than one, my major has proven to be difficult for me not just academically, but with my vision, as well. In the lab, I often struggle to read the markings on the beakers, graduated cylinders, or thermometers because I cannot see them easily. In chemistry, many of the chemicals tend to be the same color or smell, and in order to know what chemical you are using, you need to know the name. You cannot exactly taste or even sometimes smell these substances because of their hazards. More importantly, science involves many observations and critical thinking, and if I cannot see what is happening during an experiment, then how can I be a scientist? While I am extremely fortunate still to have plenty of day vision left, these are issues that I still need to address. It will perhaps mean a change of career down the road.

At times people ask me what is the most frustrating thing that I have dealt with when it comes to Usher syndrome. I can sum up my answer in three words: "lack of independence." Since I cannot drive due to Usher syndrome, I feel frustrated because I have to rely on people to take me places. Not only that, but some of my closest friends live a good forty-five minutes or more from me. I do not get to see them as often as I would like because I cannot drive, or public transportation is not accessible in their town. At times, I feel guilty that I cannot see them because I cannot drive. While not being able to drive does contribute greatly to my lack of independence, my night-blindness does play a role, as well. Here in Boston, Massachusetts, it is pitch-black by 4:00 p.m. in the afternoon during the winter. My parents do not feel comfortable with my being out at my college campus at night, even if it is a short walk to some place. I do not blame them for feeling this way, but it is still frustrating. In order for me to get anywhere at night, I would have to call Public Safety and wait ten to twenty minutes for them to come get me, while I could already be on my way over to the library.

While I am leading a wonderful life despite Usher syndrome because of the many people who have supported me throughout the years, living with Usher syndrome is still tough. Every single day, I have to face certain obstacles that other people do not have to face, such as getting around at night, getting to places, and seeing the blackboard from far away. I am fortunate though to be able to hear due to my cochlear implants. While I am only a college student, there are so many things that I want to do with my life, such as traveling, research, teaching, and creating art. I can only do those things, if I have my vision. That is why, more than anything in the world, I want a cure for Usher syndrome.

ABOUT THE AUTHOR

Jessica Chaikof was born in Atlanta, Georgia, but moved to Boston, Massachusetts, when she was fifteen and has been living there ever since. She was born profoundly deaf and later diagnosed with Usher syndrome 1F. She received her first cochlear implant at age fifteen months and was the youngest child in the United States at the time to receive one. She received a bilateral cochlear implant in 2004. She graduated from Newton North High School in 2014 and is currently a sophomore at Wheaton

College in Norton, Massachusetts, majoring in chemistry. Her hobbies include ceramics, origami, reading, and traveling. She has been to Australia, Poland, England, Czech Republic, and many other countries. Jessica is a major Harry Potter and Doctor Who fan. Currently, she is trying to live her life in the best possible way she can, while remaining hopeful for a cure for Usher syndrome someday.

CHAPTER 11

IT'S ALWAYS CHRISTMAS

WITH GREAT HUMOR AND INSIGHT, A MOTHER SHARES HER INTERIOR DECORATING TIPS ADAPTING HER HOME TO MAKE DAILY LIFE EASIER FOR HER ADULT USHER 1 SON.

KAREN DUKE

It is evening, and the Christmas lights are twinkling brightly like stars in the night. Not where you may think, like on a Christmas tree or wreath, but around the door frames and fake plants and trees strategically placed for a reason.

Believe me, I am no Christmas fanatic. Think of the lights like an airport strip, guiding the plane to its destination. This is Christmas all year 'round in our Usher home. The Christmas lights guide my adult son, all 6'2"/200 pounds of him. One too many wall crashes, articles knocked over and broken, made me think creatively: why not use Christmas lights to guide him through our home? It might look silly to some in the middle of the summer, but what the heck, they work beautifully. Thank God there is the internet for replacements because trying to find Christmas lights off-season at the local mall is impossible!

THE KITCHEN

Now the kitchen with an Usher son can be quite challenging. We both decided no stove or oven-type cooking for the handsome young bachelor. There is this invention called the crockpot that we took on with a fever, scouring the internet for interesting, tasteful recipes. Crockpot cooking is great for my Usher son– no worries about fire– it slow-cooks all day, and when I get home from work, it's all ready to eat. There is also, of course, the convenient microwave, which is used quite frequently.

Plates and glasses are a different story. We have no dishwasher, so hand-washing dishes is an everyday chore; however, with an Usher son, many of the plates and dishes get broken. It makes my dish array quite unique with all different patterns and styles and no complete sets.

Then there is the darn trashcan. Most people would think it's pretty big, huh? Not for my Usher son. I get left little surprises everyday on the floor where he missed the bucket and couldn't see that it landed on the floor.

Mom the exterminator, that's me! Thank God I am not afraid of bugs. If my son can't see a laundry basket on the floor, how the heck could he see a big brown spider or a trail of marching ants? I inspect his downstairs apartment (I live upstairs) almost daily for those little buggers. At least with my eyes at the helm we are bite-free.

YARD WORK

Care around our Usher home can be quite interesting– for example, the dreaded lawn mower. My Usher son wants to be like any other of the male species and run the lawnmower. It makes for a very interesting pattern in my lawn, like the Mohawk look, with spikes everywhere because he cannot see what he has already mowed. We switched last year to an electric mower, and you can guess how that worked out three new extension cords later!

How about the dreaded snow shoveling with the bright sun shining on the crisp, white snow piercing his Usher eyes? Add to the madness his Usher balance issues on a simple flat surface, never mind snow and ice covered. But we work together, and it eventually gets done. I clear the spaces he misses because he cannot see what the heck he shoveled and what he didn't. I call it *Usher-snow-no-perception*.

As a matter of fact, my Usher son was magnificent during our bloody relentless snowstorms in New England this past year. I was sick as a dog, had 7 feet of snow (no lie), and the laundry vent was blocked for weeks. Now that is a fire hazard waiting to happen. He went out for hours by himself, with less vision than he normally has due to the glare from that bright, white snow, shoveled the 7-foot drifts, and actually found the dryer vent—Yahoo! Pheww, we were running out of clothes. My hero!

In our Usher home I am the "Soccer Mom" even though my Usher son has never played soccer nor ever will. What really is a soccer Mom? To me it is the perpetual taxi driver running around in all different directions. Well, that would be me for my adult Usher son. State-funded transportation for the deaf/blind in our state is ridiculous, especially living in the suburbs away from public transportation. Grocery shopping, drug stores, doctor offices, social events, banking, post office, hardware store, mall, restaurants, social services, etc., etc., are the Soccer Mom's dream. Especially those last train runs at 11:30 at night with the alarm clock going off at 5:00 in the morning to go teach high school students—Yippee! Now that is a real "Soccer Mom". I have a smile on my face to greet the train close to the midnight hour and guide my son in the dark, his hand on my shoulder, to a nice warm car, to a nice warm house, safe and sound. Not too good on the beauty sleep!

Let's move on and talk about the five senses.

HEARING

The five senses are quite unique in our Usher home. Let's start with hearing. My Usher son is profoundly deaf and uses sign language to communicate. The best part is I can play my music as loud as I want, and it doesn't faze him. He doesn't know what music is, so we never have to compete for the radio station or CD in the car. I just sing along to my heart's content be-bopping along as we go. He is such a sport. He even dances with me when I'm in that dancing mood, all the while not hearing a note. His rhythm is pretty good for being deaf. He just follows my lead, rocking and swaying.

Another great relaxation tool is yelling! I can yell and yell and swear and swear up and down and he has no idea that I am ready to kill him or blow my top. I can mutter all kinds of words under my breath that he can't hear, but it makes me feel better! All kidding aside, I do so wish I could just talk to him because talking in sign language takes 10 times as long. Now with his decreasing vision, we have certain spots in the house that are easier for him to see than others so we gravitate to those spots. He shuffles me gently into just the right place for him to see me.

Now, have you ever locked your keys in the house my mistake? I have. Try getting a deaf/low vision person's attention while he's snug and warm inside, and you are freezing your tootsies off outside, locked out. I tried and tried ringing his special doorbell that flashes. However, if he is not positioned correctly due to his peripheral vision loss, he cannot for the life of him see it. I could have banged on the door until the cows came home, but he wouldn't have heard me. A stampede of elephants would have to come through his living room to get his attention. So, I went around the back of the house, got up on a patio chair, opened the upstairs bathroom window (thank God it was not locked), and crawled through that teeny-weeny space, all without him hearing a word or sound, just moseying around carefree. Meanwhile, I was ready to collapse, yet also to celebrate with bells that I got in the house!

SEEING

I do have sight advantage in some quirky instances, like hide and seek without having to hide. It is pretty easy to hide from my Usher son. He can walk right by me, and all I have to do is duck, and he never sees me. He also can't hear my footsteps, so if I want to avoid a conversation at the moment, it's duck n' hide. It is also much easier to hide those unwanted vegetables in our dinners, out of sight, out of mind.

Unfortunately, the sad part is I can't have my home the way I want it due to his visual loss. I am constantly the floor police! There are "no fly zones" in the paths throughout our Usher house, meaning, nothing on the floor at all. Even if I think that he can see something, nope, wrong again, and crash he goes. It makes for a nice tidy house though. He knows where all the furniture pieces are, but if one thing like a pair of shoes or school bag is left in one of the paths—crash!

Maybe you can guess the scariest visual moments? Our Usher house is in sheer panic mode when we lose power at night due to a storm here in New England. It is a terrifying reality of what my son's life would be like if he goes completely blind with his profound hearing loss: total darkness and total silence. He literally freezes and waits for my guided hands to tactile sign to stay calm. He waits for those reassuring, signed words: "Don't worry, sweetheart– the lights will be back on soon." It is one of those "in your face moments" that you can't deny that this may be his life someday. At the height of our distress and terror— Pop! The lights are back on, and all is well again in our Usher house.

TOUCH

Touch to me is pretty obvious, but maybe not to most. If you are around an Usher type 1 person like my son, you'd better love touching. First, let's tackle tactile signing. Tactile signing is when you sign either into the palm of a deaf/blind person or hold their hands and sign regular sign in unison, as one, together. We use the latter. My son requires tactile signing in dimly lit areas and in the dark. It is "up close and personal" and at the same time, extremely time-consuming. Regular sign language is slow enough, but tactile signing "IS" the tortoise!

Then there is the attention piece. The one pet peeve I personally have with his deafness is his inability to hear me asking him a question or just simply trying to get his attention. I literally have to get up and tap him each time or stomp on the floor so he can feel the vibration. Hearing people can shout from room to room or floor to floor. Not in our Usher home. You have to literally get up every time you want to get his attention. I look at it on the bright side: the up and down, up and down keeps me fit and trim.

Lastly, but certainly not least, is guiding. My Usher son is comfortable with holding one hand on the shoulder of his guide to get him safely to his destination. I started out by saying touch is pretty obvious, but it really is a lifeline for Usher's, so one must love to be touched—don't we all!

TASTE

What can I say about taste except that "food" is my Usher son's favorite dish! Not that I'm tooting my own horn as a good cook, but if he had his Great-Grandma Gathry for a cook, he might be "signing" a different tune about the taste of food. Thank you to my other Grandma, Barchie, and to my Mom for the tools they gave me to be a good cook to please my son's palate. It is just my opinion, but I think those with Usher have a heighted sense of taste due to their dual sensory loss of hearing and vision. Food is the one satisfying treat that makes my son forget about his Usher's as he basks in all those flavors of sweet, salty, hot, spicy, and savory!

SMELL

The last sense of interest is smell. Yikes! The nose my Usher son has! Sometimes after a long day at work, I want to sneak in the door and quickly escape upstairs to my place of solace, only to find my son hot on my trail. He can "smell" that I am home. I don't even have my coat off or school bag put away, and he is right in my space signing frantically about whatever he finds so gosh darn important at that very moment. He can pick out my perfume that I put on 7 hours prior a mile away! I don't know too many people who can do that. He can tell from downstairs that I have a different candle smell burning and runs up to ask what the name of it is. I can't sneak any snacks or lunches of my own because he smells the smallest foods cooking all the way downstairs with the upper door closed. He rushes right upstairs following his nose like a bloodhound to its prey. He's also saved my car a few times with that almost detective nose. He could smell a tiny burning sensation in the engine of my car. Of course, he was correct– anti-freeze empty! I could have burned up my engine. Saved again by that snout!

Needless to say, living in our Usher home is never boring. Ours is unique, eccentric, yet practical for deafness and blindness. Our house is complete with Christmas lights all year 'round!

ABOUT THE AUTHOR

Karen Duke currently lives in Massachusetts and is the single mother of an adult son, born in 1982, who has Usher syndrome type 1. Following his diagnosis in 1986, she enrolled in a Master's Degree program in Speech Language Pathology and has been a high school Speech Language Pathologist for the last 23 years. This chapter is dedicated to her son Randall, who has taught her to be a compassionate and patient mom to an Usher syndrome child.

PART 3

INDEPENDENT LIVING

CHAPTER 12

THE BLINDING DRIVE AND BEYOND

A YOUNG WOMAN DRIVING A CAMARO SPORTS CAR AT NIGHT SUDDENLY CANNOT SEE AND MUST COME TO TERMS WITH COPING WITH USHER... OR ELSE.

SONYA MARNEY

"I *LOVE* this!" she said. At age sixteen, driving a sporty Camaro down Highway 610 late at night, she was flush with adrenaline, her red hair seeming to float around her in her excitement. "Wow, this is so much fun!" Her boyfriend Kevin was teaching her to drive for the first time at night, and she was relishing it in pure delight. Up ahead, the freeway divided, two lanes to the left, two to the right, and two going straight. She was in one of the lanes that was shared with the left hand turn and the straight path. But terror flooded her. Something was wrong, something totally unexpected, terrifying, and life changing.

The street lights were spaced oddly, and in the darkness between them, her vision narrowed. Gone were the cars around her, her boyfriend, street signs. Fear arose within her, slowing her reaction. Speeding at 65 miles per hour, orange and black barrels swam into her narrowed view, backed by guardrails and the concrete divider. She lifted her foot off of the accelerator in reaction, and Kevin's hand turned the steering wheel, guiding the car towards the left turn, the car having drifted too far to continue on Highway 610 without meeting those barrels. She shivered in reaction. In no way could she continue to drive that night and felt that, with herself behind the wheel, she was a loaded gun in a child's hand. She was driving a deadly weapon, and woe to them who stood in front of the barrel when the trigger was pulled.

"What the hell was that?" Kevin asked breathlessly. His voice quavered in reaction, while he continued to guide the steering wheel from the passenger seat. Rocked to her very core, shaking all over, she let out a long slow breath before speaking.

"I…. I don't know. I could see and then I couldn't see. I don't understand it. I'm so sorry. I don't understand what just happened. I'm going to pull over here and you can drive me home."

****

Hi, my name is Sonya, known to my close friends and family as Sunny, and I have Usher syndrome type 2A. The experience I just shared with you is just one of many I have had on my journey thus far in my life– a journey so confusing and mind boggling that I never fully received my answers until twenty-two years after that incident.

I was a normal, healthy, and athletic young girl. I loved the outdoors, and I played until the sun started to go down. I did not have any girlfriends on the street, so all my playmates were boys my age. It was a fierce competition being the sole female playing sports and games against five to ten boys. Because I was a daredevil, if anyone told me I couldn't do something, I did it to prove that I could do it. Oh, but not just to do it, but to do it even better. Nothing could stop me from doing what I wanted, except my own bad attitude. That's how I saw life for many, many years: grab it by the horns and nothing else mattered.

Looking back, I realize that not only did I have hearing problems, but I couldn't see as well as everyone around me at night. The question is, "How did I fool everyone for so long?" I was obviously born with hearing impairment, but it was not caught until I was almost six years old. Several tests were done over the years before someone finally caught on to what a mischievous sneak I was. Well, *they* thought I was being mischievous, but I just wanted to make everyone happy. At first I was thought to be autistic because I would not focus on a person until after they got my attention, but a very lovely lady realized I was "playing games" when it came to hearing tests. Back in the '70s and early '80s, I sat in front of the audiologist giving the test and was told to raise my hand when I heard the beep. Well, I quickly realized that every time they turned that knob on the machine I was supposed to raise my hand, right? Well, no, but I did that because I wanted everyone to pat me on the back and say I was a good girl.

This audiologist caught on to my little game and had me go to a special school where they had those frightening booths. Yes, I had to sit inside a small, enclosed booth while she sat outside behind me, looking through a little glass. And, what do you know! This time the test revealed that I had a severe hearing impairment.

"But she understands us so well! How can that be?"

"She knows her words well– she just can't pronounce them well."

My parents were in a mixed state of emotions, relieved to finally know what was going on, but they also had a lot of other questions, very valid ones. I was obviously a smart little girl. I had learned how to read lips as a baby, and I still can do this almost forty years later.

When the hearing loss was diagnosed at the age of six, my speech was atrocious. A serious case of the "Only your mother could possibly understand you!" I think I only knew my vowels and six consonants by that time. Many years of daily one to two hours of speech therapy, and I talk pretty normal to this day. However, no one ever forgets me once they hear me talk. I remember one of my counselors when I was thirteen telling me, "Ms. Marney, you're such a pretty girl. You could have any boy you want here… until you open your mouth!"

Around this same time, I was over at a friend's house and there was a rather large group of us. This friend lived in the neighborhood, and his mother was blind. She would walk in the room we were in and check the light switch. If it was down, it meant it was off (obviously) and she would scold them. My friend thought he was going to be smart and put in a black light. So, of course, it was still dark when she would come in and check the light switch. "Wow, that sure is mean of them to do this to her," was my first initial thought. Then I realized that everyone else could see pretty well in the dark, but I couldn't even see my own hand in front of my face. However, it was dark, and you're not supposed to see well in the dark, right? Maybe everyone else had more experience in the dark than I did. Yeah, that's what it was.

Then, at sixteen, a near brush of a horrific accident driving at night scared me witless at the time, but I didn't think much of it. It was a fluke, a one-time incident. I continued to drive without issues for many years. There was nothing wrong with me except for my hearing impairment, but I usually could get away with it. Not many people caught on that I was hearing impaired unless they knew of someone else who also was hard of hearing or deaf.

At the age of twenty-two I had my first and only child who is the light of my life. Although there had been incidents in the past when I tripped over things in the dark and I had just laughed it off, it was now my close friends who noticed that my vision was not that great at night. Yet, it wasn't severe enough to warrant anything more than "you're such a clumsy woman" or "you're blind as a bat at night, girl" but it was all in jest. Well, so we thought.

I was twenty-nine years old when I finally had my eyes dilated for the very first time by an ophthalmologist. I was sitting there amazed at how I couldn't even see words on the wall due to the dilating medications, when in came the doctor, and she had such a sour, somber face—more than her usual resting face.

"Ms. Marney, has anyone ever told you about *retinitis pigmentosa*?" she asked me quietly.

"Retin.. Huh? What? Apparently not, I have no idea what words you just said."

"Ms. Marney, you indicate on your paperwork that you have never had your eyes dilated before, is that correct?" she asked me, with her eyebrows furrowed into almost disbelief.

"Yeah, you're right. I'm going to come in here and just lie about something so stupid like that. You got me. Busted," I said sarcastically, getting irked at her questioning me like I was a criminal or just outright a liar.

"I understand, Ms. Marney, but this is serious. Your vision is in pretty bad shape. You have the classic symptoms of *retinitis pigmentosa*, a disease of the retina that may cause you to go completely blind."

She continued talking, but everything she said after "blind" became gibberish to me. I couldn't get past that word: "blind."

I remember feeling denial, anger, and just downright wanting to be mean. But I held it in and just ignored her. She gave me a bunch of brochures about RP (*retinitis pigmentosa*). I sat in my car for an hour, waiting for my eyes to see well enough to drive, and I went to the park in my neighborhood. I sat in the car, struggling to read the pamphlets and brochures I was given. It listed the symptoms: difficulty seeing at night and a loss of peripheral vision. I laughed reading those words and thought to myself that my peripheral vision was fine and the doctor was wrong. I had just started to accept my hearing loss, finally understanding it didn't make me less of a person and it wasn't something to hide or be ashamed of. Now I am also going blind? It still shocks me when I see or hear that word.

I headed home and hugged my seven-year-old daughter. The fear in the back of my head kept saying that I might not be able to see her grow up and the despair coupled with fear almost incapacitated me. The other thing that kept slamming into me was the fact that it was hereditary. That meant my beautiful little girl could possibly have this as well. Oh, no, that made me feel guilt at a level no parent should ever feel.

I set up an appointment for my daughter that same week, two days later, and sighed with relief when the tests came back stating there were no apparent signs of RP. However, this meant she wasn't quite in the clear because it could still show up later in her life. Several tests later and at almost seventeen years of age now as I write this, she has no signs. She sees so much better than I ever did growing up.

Now, what did I do after my first initial diagnosis and having my daughter checked? I stayed in denial for the next three years.

Clearing.

Then, at age thirty-two I just couldn't ignore the constant noise in the back of my head telling me, "You should've seen that. Why didn't you? You are going blind. Admit it! Stop being a dummy and just find out for sure!" I then went to a retina specialist in the medical center, at the original ophthalmologist's referral. I was sitting there waiting for everything to begin when the doctor came in and read my chart. He said, "You're hearing impaired, Ms. Marney?"

Feeling the age old embarrassment crawl up in a red hot heat flash to my face (this guy was actually attractive), I replied sheepishly, "Yes, I am."

"Ms. Marney, has anyone ever told you that you may have Usher syndrome? It is something where you have both vision and hearing loss."

"Oh, so I may not be going blind then?" was my first sudden burst of hope.

"I didn't say that. Someone who has Usher has *retinitis pigmentosa* and is also hearing impaired."

I must have looked so crestfallen that he immediately touched my leg and assured me that everything would be okay and he would send me to another doctor to find out for sure if I had Usher syndrome. The rest of the testing, hours later, went in a blur. I just wanted to run and hide and lick my wounds. I was given the test results, "Yes, you definitely have RP, there's no doubt about that. I really want you to follow up with..." and that was it as far as I was concerned. My mind shut everything else out. I didn't want to hear. I refused to hear!

This is when I really started doing research into *retinitis pigmentosa* and Usher syndrome. I wanted to know more about this nemesis. Usher was a singer's name, for goodness' sake. But it did seem to fit me like a glove, this whole Usher business. Amidst mixture of denial and tears, with each teardrop came more acceptance of the inevitable. I started looking at life in a completely different way. Not only was I not as much of a dare devil, but I started to think that one day I may not be able to see even the sky or hear the cars on the road, the loud boom boom of music coming from them, people talking to me, or laughing.

Then I thought of the hardest thing about not being able to see or hear: my daughter. Will I miss her blossoming into a young woman, falling in love, getting married? Will I not be able to see her children, hear her children, my grandchildren? Am I going to grow old just to live in a dark world—a world I won't be able to hear, or see? I'm ashamed to admit that it took me another three years before I finally accepted that I could not run from Usher syndrome. The last straw was sitting in my spiffy cool Ford Mustang with my ten-year-old daughter sitting next to me, singing her heart out. She asked me if I could hear her sing, and all I could say was, "Well, honey, no not really. I mean, I know you're singing because I can hear some sounds coming out, but I can't really understand what you are saying." When she replied: "Man, I sure wish you could hear me sing," my heart broke into a billion gazillion pieces. Tears flooded my eyes so bad I was afraid to keep driving. My heart pounded so loud in my chest that I heard nothing but my own heartbeat for some time. Then, I decided to do something about it. It was time I heard my daughter while I still could.

The long journey to try to obtain hearing aids started again. I hadn't worn hearing aids since I was a kid. The hearing aids back then were analog and amplified what I already could hear, rather than helping me hear what I couldn't hear and needed to hear. I made an appointment with an audiologist and going through the tests, I felt a major *déjà vu*. This time I did not play any games, although I was tempted for old time's sake! She gathered the results and came up to me. She confirmed that I had moderate to severe hearing loss. Then she brought me a pair of really small hearing aids—so small that I was just shocked they could do anything but squeal in someone's ear. I put them on; she turned them on and my entire world changed, just like that. I heard the clacking of the keys on the keyboard, my fingernails on the table, her footsteps on the carpet as she walked back to her desk. I just sat there with a completely idiotic dumbfounded look on my face. Tears flooded my face and for once I didn't care if I couldn't see. I could hear! I could really hear!

The doctor also had tears in her eyes and when I asked if the world was really that noisy, she busted out laughing. Wiping her tears away, and with me doing the same, she nodded and said that it was. I honestly had no idea what I was missing out on, and I couldn't believe the difference these hearing aids made compared to the huge bulky and totally useless ones I had had when I was a kid. We both chatted, and I realized I could really hear myself talk more, so I became self-conscious of my voice. I felt like a six-year-old all over again, going to speech therapy and hating my voice.

Then came the heartbreaking news. Once again, my insurance wouldn't cover hearing aids because I was over twenty-six, and it was a pre-existing condition. I had heard this before, twice to be exact, when I tried previously to get hearing aids. "Dear God, there's got to be a way I could get hearing aids!" I said in frustration and shared my previous experiences with the doctor. She was supportive and felt that I deserved a chance to be able to hear just like anyone else. She gave me the name and number of a lady who could probably help and asked me to call her. I gave her a hard, big hug when I left. This doctor would become a person in my memory bank I would never, ever forget. The lady I was to contact worked in the communications department for DARS, Department of Assistive Rehabilitative Services.

In the midst of going through this, I had a fantastic group of co-workers who truly went above and beyond for me. I explained the situation to one of my partners on the project I was working on, and she spoke with someone else on the team about my issue. One of these beautiful people lived in another country, and he was able to get the hearing aids there for a fraction of the cost. Oh, but that's not all. This man and my lovely partner went in together on the cost and presented these hearing aids as a gift to me.

When I put them on and turned them on, I heard different sounds I hadn't heard in my entire life. I never knew projectors and the screens that came down made those noises or that the chairs we sit on made noises when we turned in them. Everything was much louder. I couldn't hug them enough for this gift. I remember choking back tears and trying not to sob like a bawling baby and trying to upkeep my professionalism. But, as soon as I got in my car and was far away from the building, the tears flowed. They were tears of joy and so much sweeter than the tears of sorrow.

I pulled over into a parking lot near home and cleaned myself up. I couldn't face my daughter wearing these hearing aids for the first time looking like a bloated, washed out ghost. Finally, I pulled up to my house and as I exited my car, I realized I could hear the birds. I walked into the house, and I heard my daughter say, "Hi, Mom!" and heard her feet come running to me to give me a hug. That experience was just so amazing. I showed her my hearing aids and told her the story of how I had obtained them. She was so excited that I could now hear her. I asked her to sing for me and sing she did, and another wave of tears and joy overcame me. My mom had a huge smile on her face– she was so happy to see them, too! That day definitely went down in the memory books for me, something I can sit back and just relive like it happened yesterday.

I continued to pursue getting hearing aids through DARS and, although it took a few extra months, these were specially designed for my hearing loss. Amazingly, all the sounds I couldn't hear before in either the hearing aids I tried on at the audiologist's office or the ones I was gifted, I could suddenly hear. It was startling to go from only hearing about 40% to almost 70%, which was a huge difference. What scared me was that there was still 30% I could not hear, but I couldn't really miss what I never had had.

During this difficult but enlightening transition of accepting what I had, I lost what I thought were true friends. But, I gained so many more through support groups on Facebook. Of all places, Facebook became my true beacon of sanity. I found other women who were going through similar emotions or had been through it, and their astounding advice touched my heart.

I have had a good career working for several companies in the accounting department, accounts payable/receivable, and most recently as a financial manager. Over the years I noticed I could no longer see the whole screen of the monitors. I was struggling to find the mouse pointer and struggling to make sure I didn't make mistakes. I would devise other programs or checklists to catch anything I missed. I was fortunate to have a couple of bosses along the way who were truly good people and tried their best to work with me in any way they could by providing the needed accommodations, such as extra large dual monitors and a special Bluetooth phone that would work with my hearing aids; and on really bad weather days I could work from home. However, over time even with accommodations, the stress of my job and trying to make sure I did what I used to do became hard to deal with. I was so distraught thinking I would be fired for, well, for not being able to be as good as I used to be. Still, I will cherish forever the bosses who worked with me and my disabilities.

When asked how having Usher syndrome has changed me, I can't help but reflect and realize that in many ways my disabilities have made me a much better person, more kind and understanding, and compassionate towards humans and animals. It has also taught me to see the best in people. This journey has also affected my whole family. I can't even fathom how to describe how my parents must feel thinking they passed these genes onto me, which was proven through a DNA test via blood work from all three of us. Both were shocked and apologetic when the results came in and I shared the information with them. I told them, like I have told everyone else, it is not their fault. Simply put, I don't regret my life. I don't regret being born. Life may be a little different for me and maybe it's more challenging than for some, but not as challenging as for others.

ABOUT THE AUTHOR

Sonya Marney was raised in Houston, Texas. She dropped out of high school in the 9th grade and eventually earned her G.E.D. Her work career started at age 18 as a filing clerk (quality control) with Continental Emsco. Over the next few years she held various positions in the accounting field including: Accounts Payable and Payroll for an environmental company, Collections for a newspaper (Greensheet), and Accounts Receivables for a medical insurance company. At Key Energy for General Ledger, she obtained supervisor and managerial experience to carry through to Weatherford, where she ended her career as a Financial Manager, almost twenty years later.

Sonya has done volunteer work through her church and community. This includes feeding the homeless, providing them with hygienic items, etc. She hopes to pursue a degree in Psychology to fulfill her dream of being a counselor for the disabled. Currently she resides in the Houston area with her daughter.

CHAPTER 13

BEING INDEPENDENT WITH USHER

"I COME FROM A FAMILY WHERE ALL WOMEN ARE WARRIORS, AND I INTEND TO DO THE SAME," WRITES THE AUTHOR, A NATIVE OF MEXICO. BILINGUAL IN ENGLISH AND SPANISH, SHE SHARES HER TIPS ON HOW TO ADAPT AS AN INTERNATIONAL IT PROFESSIONAL, AND HOW TO SUCCEED IN LIVING A FULFILLING LIFE IN SPITE OF USHER AND RETINITIS PIGMENTOSA.

DIANA VELARDE

Growing up, one usually has a lot of dreams and hopes that someday they will come true. My dreams have included the classic ones: finding love, starting a family, becoming a successful professional, traveling, studying abroad, and, of course, changing the world. Other things that are sometimes taken for granted and are not included in the wish list are peace, health, independence, happiness, and stability. When I was growing up I simply wanted to be happy and to have life go smoothly. Of course, as adults we learn from life experiences, and that usually makes us change our goals and desires. I am now thirty-two years old and have achieved some of my goals, including studying abroad, and I have given up others, such as driving, but I have also added new ones like learning archery. What I never thought was that I would embrace independence in a way I never imagined.

I'm not naïve. I was diagnosed with bilateral sensorineural hearing loss when I was seven years old, even though my parents knew there was something wrong at an even younger age. I started wearing hearing aids, and I grew up with some expected difficulties as I learned to cope with my limitation. Being a teenager is difficult; add a disability, and the confusion and frustration increase. Still, I was fine, and I would say I had a "normal" childhood. I experienced successes that no one expected, such as being a top student, although doctors had told my parents I wouldn't go beyond secondary school. By the time I moved to another city to go to university at the age of seventeen, I had faced various situations related to my hearing loss. I thought I already knew all the problems I could have being hearing impaired, and I sensed life would not be easy, but it would be manageable. University life was actually really good. I excelled academically, made new friends, and I fell in love for the first time.

Reality hit me in my early twenties as I realized that life would bring more challenges. The first time I noticed any problems with night vision was at the age of nineteen during a faith outreach program when it became difficult for me to get around at night. That caught my attention because I had also attended when I was fifteen and seventeen, and I didn't have any issues then. Still, I was not officially diagnosed with *retinitis pigmentosa* (RP) until I was twenty-five. Accepting it wasn't easy, and I fell into depression. After a few years of therapy and with the support of my family and friends, I accepted my RP with renewed faith. Seven years later, I now accept my limitations, but the war isn't over. New battles will come, I will cope with new emotions, and I will strive to not fall into depression again.

Today, I am in many ways a normal young woman who likes dancing, shopping for shoes and clothes, and eating junk food, and who dreams about meeting her Mr. Darcy in a sweetly romantic way. I enjoy hanging out and talking to my family and friends. My professional career is very important to me, and for me, the best workplace is one where I like what I do.

My vision loss, however, has progressed significantly in the last seven years. I have no remaining peripheral vision, and I am night blind. I perceive spots of blurriness in the limits of my visual field, but generally my central vision is considered to be fine by my retina specialist. I have Cystoid Macular Edema (CME), and I am treated for it, with ups and downs of improvement. On the bad days the vision feels blurrier. The hearing loss has been stable for the last eleven years, and I continue to wear hearing aids. My hearing ability without them is around 15% and, as is often the case with autosomal recessive disorders, I am the only one in my family who has Usher syndrome.

So far, it is mostly my hearing loss issues that affect the professional side of my life, while the other aspects of my life are affected more by the visual impairment part of Usher syndrome. There are situations where the dual sensory loss makes things worse. One of the most obvious is being at a party with dim light, loud music, and lots of people moving around. For me, it is overwhelming, and it feels like I have lost touch with reality in a bad way, not being able to hear or see. It can be quite tiring dealing with it. I will briefly discuss the impact of Usher syndrome on the professional and personal parts of my life.

PROFESSIONAL CAREER

In the ten years of my professional career, one of the toughest challenges I have faced has been the English language. A Mexican in the era of globalization is required to know English in my field: IT, consulting, and more recently, as an advisor in mergers and acquisitions. My difficulty with the language is not due to a lack of preparation, given that I studied English from elementary school to the university level, had private lessons, studied English as a second language in Canada for four months, and earned a postgraduate degree in the United Kingdom. I speak English fluently and, despite my accent, native speakers still understand me. However, I do rely on lip-reading to understand what others are saying, which makes my listening skills very weak. I find that I need lip-reading more with English than with Spanish, my native language.

The problem usually starts during the application process for a job. Today it is quite common to have initial interviews performed over the phone, and the knowledge of English is tested then. I have applied for jobs in different countries, including

Mexico. Unfortunately, not many companies offer accommodations, even though I disclose my hearing disability, and I ask for video calls or face-to-face interviews. Thus, I have been rejected because I cannot have a proper conversation in English over the phone. This rejection brought me many tears in the past, but I acknowledge I was really not the best candidate for some of the positions because they required frequent communication over the phone in English with clients or peers. Nevertheless, it is frustrating to see that my career's progress is slowed down due to Usher syndrome.

In other cases I have not been selected for some jobs because of my hearing impairment rather than my English skills. Having passed all the interviews, I was once rejected after a health checkup that included a regular hearing test in Spanish. It was disappointing that a multinational company could discriminate in the twenty-first century while claiming to provide an equal opportunity. I don't disclose my visual impairment during the application process because it does not affect my ability to perform a job at this point. I simply do not apply for jobs that require me to drive.

There are companies, however, that have given me accommodations during the application process and have even offered me a job knowing about my disability. While it can be tough for disabled persons to get a job, I acknowledge there are equal opportunity firms out there that support employees with disabilities, and those are the places where I want to work. My previous and current employers are examples of responsible and accommodating firms.

USHER ACCOMMODATIONS ON THE JOB

What is the day-to-day experience like at my job? Let's take my current job as an example. My manager knew about my hearing issues when she hired me, and she has supported me in that sense. Little by little, my peers have become aware of my hearing impairment, and I have let them know that I need help sometimes. Indeed, I cannot hide that I have a hearing issue because of my voice tone that is easily picked up. My hearing aids are rarely visible, as I usually wear my hair down to cover them. I am not embarrassed, but I prefer that people don't judge me or get a negative first impression based on the need for hearing aids.

During a call or a conference in English, I cannot be alone, and I always ask for a summary of what was said. I take notes of visual information such as slides and, if possible, ask others to share their notes. Also, during calls I sit close to the phone to try to pick out key words. Fortunately, my workplace functions in a project-scheme, which means that usually I have at least one teammate present. My hearing ability, in general, is limited, so communicating via email, chat, and using a telephone with extra high volume are ways to compensate without requiring further accommodations. During meetings I try to sit in the middle where I can hear everyone and read their lips. For training, I try to sit in the first row, something I started doing during my student years. Still, sometimes I have to ask others to repeat what they said.

Although RP still does not interfere with my ability to do my job, I eventually disclose it to my colleagues for several reasons. Having tunnel vision, I can be seen as a rude person when someone tries to shake hands with me or approaches and I don't notice it. I can also appear to be a clumsy person when I run into obstacles or bump into other people by accident because I could not see them. When someone points at something and I have no idea where they are pointing, I need help as well. Sometimes it seems to take forever to find the pen that I accidentally dropped in front of me, and I need assistance. Perhaps the most important reason for disclosure is that at any point I could be in a situation where it is dark or there is low-lighting, and I will absolutely need their help. As an example, last year our group was taken to a hotel at the beach during a three-day annual strategic conference. Cocktails and dinners were served outdoors every evening, and I had two choices: either ask for help, or risk falling into any of the swimming pools that were everywhere around the hotel. I love to swim but because I wear hearing aids I cannot afford to get them wet!

Of course, I still have had embarrassing moments. One time, I was with my colleagues in a dark restaurant for a dinner that was organized by my manager. We had been there for a while when a man stood behind me. I thought he was a waiter, so I asked him for another drink. It turned out to be a director whom I was asking for a whiskey, and I wanted the earth to swallow me!

To manage my visual impairment at work, I use magnification tools on my laptop and smartphone. When there is a presentation, I also have to consider the position of the screen before deciding where to sit. As a safety measure, I carry a flashlight in my bag at all times in case I need more light.

There might be people who think that I should accept my limitations with English and move on to a different career. However, I come from a family where all women are warriors, and I intend to do the same. I cannot conceive my life to be different in that sense. I will stay with my career because it is what I like and am qualified to do. I am afraid of the day when my visual impairment will affect my ability to perform a job, forcing me to disclose both impairments during the application process. Yet, I hope to continue working for at least fifteen more years, and I will also start looking for options for home employment so I don't have to stop working until retirement age.

PERSONAL SIDE

One of the consequences of RP as it progresses is gradually becoming dependent on others. It started with my needing help from others to get around after dark. Now it is more and more frequent that I need to ask someone to take me to the restroom in a public place, to let me hold his/her arm to get around in a crowded place even in the daytime, or to navigate stairs I'm not familiar with, especially going down. I suppose that most individuals with Usher syndrome fight against that dependency, but when one starts struggling more and more, asking for help becomes the obvious solution. It took many bumps and bruises in the forehead and knees to accept that I had to do something. I still think that signs, trees, furniture, and other things just love to stand in my way. I know that I'm not the only one who hates the wet floor signs, as there is no way a person with narrow visual field can know it is there waiting to trip one.

I'm aware there will always be a degree of dependency and that it will only increase over time, but I believe there are lots of things I can do to be relatively independent. A few years ago, I lived with my siblings, and we decided to move somewhere else. I asked them if we could choose a place that was located near stores and major streets, where I could easily walk and access transportation. They were totally supportive, and we found a house with those characteristics. Today, I live alone in Mexico City, one of the most populated cities in the world, and I moved there with the goal of living within walking distance to my job. While I am thankful for the support from friends who in the past picked me up every day from home to go to work, it makes me feel happy to know I don't need anyone to take me to work. I have found that the key to achieving independence is to accept my limitations and find ways to adapt and deal with these issues. Thus, I'd rather be independent and live in an accessible place than have a pretty house in a suburb where I cannot go anywhere unless someone picks me up.

SOCIALIZING

To go out and have a social life, if possible, I rely on my close friends. The rest of the time if I have to go to a place I am not familiar with, if possible, I go there in the daytime to familiarize myself with it before attending the evening social event. I use online maps to study the streets I might cross. The street view in the maps is also very useful to try to find a place in advance, instead of struggling to find it in the evening.

For a night out, I only attend if I know there will be someone I trust to help me find the restroom and help me get around safely.

This becomes challenging when I have just met a new group of people. In those cases, I drink little or no alcohol, and I leave early. I have the phone numbers of taxi companies on my cellphone so that I can call a cab without having to walk down the street to find one. Thus, the recent apps for smartphones that allow requesting a taxi are amazing. I find that I literally memorize the route to places where I go more often. For example, I know the way to my workplace very well, including the location of obstacles like trees, sidewalks, and stairs. When I have to walk through a place I don't know in the evening, I walk ridiculously slowly using my feet to feel the changes in the terrain and the obstacles. Obviously, flat shoes are more appropriate in these situations, so I give up wearing high heels more often than I would like to.

DATING

Having Usher syndrome and dating can be challenging, as guys could feel intimidated when they learn that I have Usher syndrome and all its implications in my life. When to disclose it becomes a reason to be nervous. A first date requires even more planning. If I am not familiar with the meeting place, do I ask the guy to take me to the restroom, or do I take a chance and go by myself, possibly hitting many things on the way and having the guy wonder if I drank too much? This all could be avoided by going out only during the daytime, going to a familiar place, and not drinking alcohol. I don't know what works best because I don't have much experience dating, but I have decided to let things happen the way they should instead of worrying. I have faith that I will find someone amazing who can see beyond the disability and can appreciate me for the person I am.

FRIENDS AND FAMILY

The confidence my family has in me has been invaluable. I am independent today because they avoided overprotecting me in the past. For example, when I moved to a much larger city to attend college, my mom was terrified about me crossing streets and not hearing a car approach. She didn't express that fear to me, and neither she nor my father tried to stop me from going away. In fact, they encouraged me to go, as they knew it was the best thing for me. My sister was already living in that city, and during the first days, she escorted me while I learned the layout of the area.

Now that I have RP issues in addition to the hearing problem, my family and friends have taken the same attitude and support me. When they are with me, they hold my arm. They are there if I need help. The rest of the time they treat me as a normal person and respect my individuality and independence even though I know they worry. Having that space helps me remain positive and confident as I go through all the struggles and embrace independence. If I fall down, if I say something inappropriate because I misinterpreted a question, if someone is rude, or I don't get a job, I might cry, pray, talk to my friends and family, or go to therapy. Then I try to learn, accept, adapt, and, if I can, laugh about all those "RP/Usher moments".

FINAL THOUGHTS

I have faith that I will live long enough to see a cure for Usher, but in the meantime, I hope to remain independent as long as I can and challenge myself by doing things that may sound trivial, but for me they are a huge success. One example is going to the theatre or to the cinema alone. Another one is travelling alone, a big challenge when you aren't familiar with the destination city. Even everyday things that sighted people do can be a challenge for me, such as walking at night through a street that I'm not familiar with and not falling down– *that* is an achievement. Remind me to tell you about the time I fell into a dumpster!

I still have dreams, and I have also given up some of them. For me, the key to managing life with Usher syndrome has been to remain independent through acceptance and adaptation. I understand that I will have to continue to adapt and make changes in the future as my sight gets worse. However, I will keep seeking new ways to remain as independent as I can possibly be. In the near future, I will start using a folding white cane, especially at night. I'm excited about the idea of having a guide dog one day, hoping that it will be a great companion and help me navigate through places. I will not deny that I am scared of the idea that if I lose more sight I will not be able to read lips, aggravating my listening skills and further affecting my life. Still, I will not give up, and I will find a workaround. I just hope someone will let me know if my Mr. Darcy is in front of me—I might not see him!

ABOUT THE AUTHOR

Diana Velarde was born in Monclova, Mexico, and currently resides in Mexico City. She was diagnosed with hearing impairment as a child. The symptoms of *retinitis pigmentosa* (RP) appeared in her early twenties, leading to a diagnosis of Usher syndrome type 2. In 2004 she earned a Bachelor of Science degree in Electronic Systems Engineering from Tecnológico de Monterrey, a top private university in Mexico. Eight years later she earned a Master of Business at Newcastle University (UK), graduated with distinction, and received the Best Student Award. With ten years of experience, today she works for a global professional services firm as an advisor in Mergers and Acquisitions (M&A) and Information Technology (IT). Diana loves reading and travelling, and her dream is to visit many more places. Her philosophy of life is represented by the quote: "If you cry because the sun has gone out of your life, your tears will prevent you from seeing the stars." (Rabindranath Tagore) But as her RP doesn't allow her to actually see stars, she prays for a cure to see them again. This story is dedicated to her parents Javier and Marisela, and her siblings Lizza and Javier, who have given her the strength to be who she is.

CHAPTER 14

TRANSITIONING WITH USHER SYNDROME

"WOULD YOU RATHER BE BLIND OR DEAF?" WAS A SURVEY QUESTION IN JUNIOR HIGH SCHOOL. YEARS LATER, WITH THE HELP OF A LEADER DOG, THE AUTHOR MAKES THE TRANSITION FROM LIVING SIGHTED TO BEING DEAFBLIND.

SHARON JAMES

I still remember years ago in junior high when one of my classmates conducted a poll for a school project entitled "Would you rather be blind or deaf?" I laughingly replied, "Neither," but was informed that I had to pick one or the other. I chose deaf, as I was already moderately hard of hearing. My reasoning was that I could always lip read or even learn sign language if it came to being totally deaf, but being blind? No way! How in the world would one be able to function at all without any vision? The only blind people I had ever seen were on TV and were portrayed as bumbling, helpless people, always groping around and dependent on others for every little task.

When I was very young, my parents didn't suspect that I had a hearing loss and just thought that I was in my own little world and that was why I didn't respond when called. They would usually send my sister to get my attention and/or tell me what was said. Without even realizing it, I must have compensated with lip reading and actually functioned quite well until the fourth grade, when I had a very soft-spoken teacher and my grades began to fall due to not being able to hear the lessons. My parents then took me to an audiologist in downtown Little Rock, Arkansas, where I was diagnosed with a bilateral moderate hearing loss and was fitted with two hearing aids. What was then believed to be hearing loss due to a side effect of high doses of streptomycin prescribed for a severe case of measles would be part of the Usher syndrome diagnosis many years later.

At the time when I started wearing hearing aids, only analog hearing aids were available, and they amplified all noises, not just the important speech sounds. I remember being taken outside next to a very busy intersection to test the new aids. The sheer loudness completely overwhelmed me and left me in tears and unwilling to wear them. Thus, even though I had a bilateral hearing loss, the doctor decided that at least in the beginning, I could only tolerate the sounds from one hearing aid. Even the noise from one hearing aid was somewhat overwhelming after years of muted hearing, but at the same time, I was so proud and excited to get back to school to show it off to my classmates. The only problem was that they didn't see it as "cool." They saw it as "different," and many just ridiculed me.

This started the pattern of hiding my hearing loss by always making sure my hair covered the hearing aid and making jokes or excuses when I wasn't able to hear things. I even stopped wearing it during my entire junior year of high school because I was a cheerleader and worried someone would see my hearing aid during my routines and jumps. I found out later that some of my classmates viewed me as aloof and even "stuck up," but the real truth was that I just didn't hear them. Somehow, through stubbornness and determination, I still managed to do well in school that year.

After that experience in fourth grade, I learned pretty quickly that some people had the same warped view of the deaf or hard of hearing that I had of the blind. I know, it may sound ridiculous, but the fact that I had somehow become embarrassed or even ashamed of being "different" by wearing a hearing aid was very real to me.

Not long ago, I read a great definition that put words to my feelings of inadequacy: "Shame is the intensely painful feeling or experience of believing that we are flawed and therefore unworthy of love and belonging. It's the fear that something we've done or failed to do, an ideal that we've not lived up to, or a goal that we've not accomplished makes us unworthy of connection." (Brené Brown)

Hearing aid technology continued to improve over the years. By the time I reached high school, new noise reduction filters had been introduced to analog hearing aids. I had taken piano lessons since early childhood, but until ninth grade when I got one of those new hearing aids, I had not truly heard the distinct notes I was playing. What an amazing experience this was! It still remains a vivid memory to this day.

Looking back on my childhood, I can't recall any difficulties I had that would suggest any type of visual impairment. However, I must have had some sensitivity to the bright sunlight because most of my childhood's outdoor pictures usually ended up with me squinting, covering my eyes, and in tears. All through my elementary and secondary years, I was actively involved in church camps and school activities with no apparent visual field or night vision limitations.

It wasn't until I was in college that I first noticed that I had trouble with glare from oncoming headlights while driving at night. I still wasn't having any other visual issues, so I just tried to limit my nighttime driving. Finally, sometime after I graduated from college, I nearly went off the road and into a ditch trying to avoid oncoming headlights that appeared as if they were coming straight toward me. That incident scared me enough to go to an ophthalmologist and see if I needed glasses.

Roughly ten years had passed from that junior high survey to the time when I was officially diagnosed with *retinitis pigmentosa* (RP) during what was to be a routine eye exam. Up until then, doctors had concluded that my hearing loss was caused by nerve damage from a severe case of childhood measles and/or high doses of streptomycin, so when they said that I had RP based on some pigments in the retina, I figured this was also due to damage from the measles. Surely it wasn't a coincidence that I already had a hearing loss and now I had a disease that caused blindness? They had to be connected, right? And the logical connection in my mind was that a bad case of measles caused the damage in both instances. There, it's settled. Doctors don't know everything, and I wasn't blind. I mean, well, blind people couldn't see like I could. Blind people groped around, ran into walls, tripped over things, and I wasn't doing that. In fact, everything looked perfectly normal to me. Yet, I realized many years later that denial is a very powerful emotion.

Not only had I been diagnosed with RP, I was told my visual field was already down to 25 degrees, and I was given a prognosis of blindness by age 40. That diagnosis was confusing to me, as I had not been having any other vision issues other than the headlights' glare.

As time passed, I learned just how adaptable humans could be. In the case of some types of Usher syndrome, where the peripheral vision loss can progress slowly over time, we often compensate by scanning the surroundings to see the whole picture. The brain is so remarkable that it mentally fills in pieces of the missing picture, which fools us into thinking we see more than we actually do. This "trick" lulls many of us to continue doing some things, such as driving, far longer than we should, not only for our safety, but everyone else's in our path.

It was when I was around 28 years old and my job required me to travel internationally that I became aware of other nighttime difficulties. Being in unfamiliar surroundings and having late night work hours, I started stumbling over curbs and steps. I would explain to my coworkers that I had some night blindness and have them help me maneuver up the steps back to my room each night. I was still unaware of any difficulties with daytime travel at that time.

My visual field remained stabilized at about 20 degrees during most of my children's school years. I was only working part time so that I could be involved in the kids' school and sports activities. I remember times when I would be walking down the school hallway and out of nowhere (it seemed), a small child would appear and, of course, I would end up plowing that poor child down. These incidents always made me feel terrible, so I began to request my volunteer projects to be grading papers, making copies, or anything else that allowed me just to stay in one place. At work, my co-workers would always comment on how focused I was on my work, as they'd have been standing in front of me for some time trying to get my attention. I just didn't see them there until they finally cleared their throats or said my name, causing me to nearly jump out of my chair. It became a joke around the office, and instead of telling them I had tunnel vision, I just laughed along with them. Even with these incidents, as well as the continuing loss of night vision, I still felt totally competent to drive to school, work, and all my kids' activities.

As the years passed, my visual field continued slowly to narrow and mobility became an issue. My children were grown and gone, and I began finally to acknowledge that I really did have RP. I still drove only in familiar places, and only close to home, thus fooling myself into thinking that since I was aware of my vision loss, I was even more careful than the average sighted driver. These thoughts are obviously pure foolishness and portray denial, but as I said before, denial is a very powerful emotion to overcome. It took my youngest son to convince me that I was not only endangering myself, but others as well. He gave me the tough love I needed when he firmly, but lovingly, told me he wanted me safe and around for a long time. As hard as it was to give up driving, I hung up the keys for good.

Though I had officially known I had RP for over 20 years, the thought of being legally blind or needing any kind of mobility assistance had still not occurred to me. I just didn't feel like I had that big of a problem. I still wasn't doing that much tripping or knocking down too many kids. Looking back, I think I must have had a very attentive guardian angel, or maybe I was just lucky not to have had any serious accidents. My luck ran out on one of our vacations when I decided to go on a walk by myself while the rest of the family went skiing. My walk started out uneventful, but to get to my destination, I had to walk through a dark building. My eyes did not adjust to this darker environment fast enough, and I took a step into the air, totally missing six steps. Somehow I landed on my feet, jarring my knees and hips, but not injuring myself in a major way. I then knew that I was missing far more than I thought, and that I needed to look into ways to travel more safely.

At 14 degrees of remaining visual field, I signed up for Orientation & Mobility (O&M) training through the Texas Commission for the Blind (now Department of Assistive and Rehabilitative Services/DARS). As soon as I learned that my instructor was planning to have me walk blindfolded through the mall on my very first outing, I bolted. No thanks. I hadn't even revealed my diagnosis to anyone but my family and closest friends, so there was no way I was going to walk around with a blindfold on, carrying a long straight white cane in such a public place as the mall! I quit before I even started.

During this time, I had a home-based entrepreneurship in business support systems, so I buried myself in my work, rarely needing to leave my office. Since my central vision was still intact, I could successfully complete the work without dealing with mobility issues. When I went to church, I would hold my husband's arm. When I went shopping with family, I would just watch their feet and follow them.

Several more years passed, and I lost more visual field. I knew it was time to try O&M training again to learn to travel totally independently. This time I had a very compassionate and patient O&M instructor who let me learn the different skills at my own pace. Although reluctant at first, I finally relented to learning to use the white cane while blindfolded. I will admit that I was terrified each and every time I put that blindfold on, but she was always there, always reassuring me and keeping me safe until I learned the skills I needed to independently travel from place to place. Three-fourths of the way into the training when I was learning to listen to the surge of the traffic before crossing the street, my instructor decided it wasn't safe for me to continue blindfolded. She observed that I was not always able to hear the direction the traffic was flowing and had almost stepped out in front of cars several times. She then suggested that I might want to consider getting a guide dog for safer travel.

During and after my training, I just couldn't bring myself to use the cane around my family or peers. I still hadn't shed those same feelings of shame and embarrassment of being "different" that I had had with wearing a hearing aid, only now, it wasn't just being hearing impaired and wearing a hearing aid, it was also being vision impaired and needing a guide dog. Also, in my mind, I could still see pretty well except for those unexpected steps or curbs. It just felt like I was faking blindness when I could get around just fine in familiar places without the use of any mobility aids. But, the trouble was that those familiar places made up a small part of my world, and I soon began to feel isolated because I feared venturing out to new places. I knew I had to take action in order to continue getting around safely.

Therefore, not long after I completed O&M training, I researched and then applied for a guide dog at Leader Dogs for the Blind in Rochester, Michigan. I was accepted and spent 26 days of intensive training with my Leader Dog O'Neesi. Meeting O'Neesi for the first time was love at first sight. She hesitantly and shyly walked into the room where I was waiting to meet her, but as soon as I dropped to my knees to talk to her, she was all over me as if we had known each other forever. She was a much faster walker than I was and struggled with dog distraction issues, but over the years we've worked together, we have synced our pace, and she has conquered her distraction issue. Having a guide dog is a lot of work, but well worth it. It's quite an experience to have a constant companion who keeps you safe and loves you unconditionally.

Coming home with a guide dog was my official "coming out" party. Many people knew I had some type of vision issue, but I was a master at pretending to be sighted. The advantage of still having good central vision was to be able to see people's reactions when I showed up with a guide dog. Basically, this was the beginning of a new life for both my husband and me.

Even though I addressed the mobility issue with the help of the guide dog, I still resisted learning other skills for the visually impaired, such as braille, the use of magnifiers, and accessibility computer software. I still pretended to be sighted, and I somewhat hid behind my fear of being "different."

Going blind gradually is a challenging journey, but slowly, I'm learning not to hide behind my fears and instead do things out of my own comfort zone. Quite often, it is the pride of not wanting to look blind that gets in the way, but I'm learning it's in my best interest to try to find different ways to do what I love to do rather than giving in to fear.

I have found that a way to deal with Usher syndrome is to find good support groups. Before the internet and online social groups, meeting anyone else with Usher syndrome was rare. For me, joining low vision support groups on Facebook and MDJunction has been a lifesaver in dealing with fear, isolation, and loneliness. I have also been fortunate to have personally met many of these online friends through various social events. Sometimes just knowing I'm not alone and that there are others out there successfully living with Usher syndrome is a great motivator.

If I had to pick just two of my biggest challenges of losing my visual field, I would choose giving up driving and the loss of independence that it implies. Having the freedom to go alone when and where I want to go has been a difficult transition. Asking others for help has proven to be a very humbling experience for me and it's something I still struggle with even years after giving up driving. Although I may not have the same type of independence I once had, I am still the same independent and capable person I once was—different, but yet the same.

Having the slow, progressive type of Usher syndrome requires repeated transitions to a new "normal." Just when we adjust to a new stage of visual field loss, we lose more, and the transition starts all over. I've even heard some who have late stage RP express that they wish they would just lose all their vision so that the need to transition would cease. I will never wish for that. I am grateful for every tiny degree of vision I have left. While I will accept and adjust to total blindness should that ever happen, I will never give up hope for a treatment or cure. Ask me today what my answer would be to that junior high poll I took so long ago, and my answer remains the same: "Neither!"

ABOUT THE AUTHOR

Sharon James resides in North Texas with her husband of thirty-four years and her six-year-old Leader Dog O'Neesi. She is the proud mother of four grown children and has five grandchildren. Born with moderate hearing loss, she was diagnosed with *retinitis pigmentosa* in 1977 and then reclassified as Usher syndrome type 2A through genetic testing in 2014. Sharon received a Bachelor of Science degree in Business, and her career fields include computer-generated visual design, graphic design/marketing, and business support services entrepreneur. She retired in 2011 and does volunteer work through her church and community.

CHAPTER 15

THE POWER OF THE CANE

WHO SAYS CANE TRAINING CAN'T BE FUNNY? SOME OF THE MOST UNIQUE IDEAS EVER ON WHAT TO DO WITH A WHITE CANE.

RANDALL DEWITT

When you see a cane, what do you envision? There could be a lot of answers—a walking cane for old people, a sugar cane that gets chopped for grains of sugar, a candy cane at Christmas, or a cane that a blind person swings like crazy. I have had pleasant experiences with the middle two. Who doesn't like sugar or candy? That leaves us with the crazy swinging cane, or what I like to call, the *Power of the Cane*.

You may wonder why would I need such a cane? Unfortunately, I have a terrible disease called Usher syndrome, which is a combination of hearing and vision loss. I was born profoundly deaf and use sign language, which places me in the type 1 category of Usher. Type 2s are usually people who are born with some hearing and speech, and some of these people may lose hearing later in life.

I didn't start losing significant vision until around the age of thirty. It is rather difficult to get used to. I rely completely on my sense of vision to communicate and experience the world, in place of my nonexistent sense of hearing. I use sign language, pen and paper, or typing back and forth to communicate with people depending on their preferred mode of communication. Just figuring out what type of communication system I can use with whom takes time and energy. It depends on if the person is hearing, deaf, or hard of hearing. Do they know sign language or don't they know sign language? Can they type or not type? Can they use pen and paper or not? All these prerequisites come into play even before the conversation has even started. All three modes require visual awareness and stimuli.

Losing my independent mobility is very difficult for me to accept. Mobility, to me, means being able to get from place to place in the community on my own. The cane is a low-tech tool to help people with their mobility who are either low vision or totally blind. I only began to learn and experience using the cane in the past couple of years.

CANE TRAINING 101

I thought I could just grab the cane and then start swinging it like crazy and call myself a cane expert. Just swinging it side to side doesn't look hard, does it? Little did I know that it would be much more complicated.

There were three significant challenges learning cane traveling. First, I was being thrust headfirst into completely new ways of dealing with very easy tasks I'd done my whole life without even thinking, like walking down a sidewalk. Second, my mobility trainer had literally zero experience with a "deaf" visually impaired person learning to use a cane. All her clients were "hearing" and visually impaired. The third aspect was the communication factor. Being deaf meant not being able to communicate without my hands, which were otherwise busy handling my cane.

When I walk down the street, normally I would just look at the ground so as to avoid tripping over things like litter, potholes, fallen limbs, or other obstacles. I would also keep my eyes constantly scanning to the sides for opening doors and people walking by me. I had to twist and swivel my neck around constantly, like a Big Papi bobble doll (I do love my Red Sox). With cane training, I had to just let go. My trainer told me to keep my head up and eyes straight ahead. That was rather difficult to do, going against a couple decades of deeply ingrained mobility actions and habits. I had to put my trust into a simple stick, relying on this inanimate object to save me from injury or even worse, death.

My mobility trainer had always worked with hearing blind people, and did not have to think about the deaf aspect of deaf-blindness. There are a lot of things hearing blind people can do that a deaf-blind person cannot in terms of mobility. Hearing blind people can hear oncoming cars. They can hear doors opening. They can converse with people behind or ahead of them. They can vocalize, "I'm sorry" or "I need some help, please." They can hear things scrape across the ground. They can hear machinery like escalators and elevators whir and beep. I constantly asked my trainer how I would incorporate mobility awareness around my deafness once I was fully blind. She could not come up with an answer for how to substitute sound-based solutions that her hearing clients use.

One day in the future a scenario may be that I walk down a sidewalk with my cane and have to put my full trust in it, with maybe no sight at all. I can envision it now: One sunny day I decide to take a walk with my cane going to my left, when suddenly a door opens onto the sidewalk on my right. I walk right into the door, shattering the glass. I immediately get tackled by people acting like attack dogs. There could be a hundred people screaming their heads off mere inches from my ears, and I would have no clue those yellers ever existed because I can't see and I can't hear. Abruptly, I get yanked like a rag doll by an angry cop trying to arrest me for breaking that door. Still no clue what is going on, except all the pushes, shoves, and roughing up like a wrestling TV show.

Rewind to today in the real world. I asked my mobility instructor what I should do in this scenario. She told me to watch out for the doors, but I countered with "What if I'm fully blind? I can't exactly see the doors or hear them open, can I?" (Awkward silence), writing stopped, continued silence, no answer!

Another example of this kind of situation is crossing a street. A hearing blind person can hear an oncoming car, and wait until there are no car noises before crossing the street. I cannot hear a car at all. Assuming I have either severe vision loss or total blindness, I would not be able to see or hear any cars coming down the street, even with headlights on. For all I know, the road could be as busy as Times Square, or as dead as a dirt road in the middle of an Iowa farm.

Another scenario: one day, I start crossing the street. Screech!—A sudden burst of intense sharp pain, and then abrupt nothingness. A couple hours later, a police officer shows up at my mother's house with a message. "I regret to inform you that your son has been in an accident."

Rewind to real life once again. I asked my instructor how I could cross the street if I cannot see the cars or their headlights, and cannot hear their approach or departure. She struggled with an answer, and ultimately couldn't come up with a practical mobility solution.

Despite her inability to answer my deaf-related mobility questions, I was still able to learn the basics. I am still grateful that I got the training from her. Without her, I would not have gotten the cane, the experiences I had with it, and the extra equipment like binoculars. The cane basics included using the cane to feel the different ground textures and how to feel my way around or over obstacles that I give nicknames to.

Traffic cones are "Dunce Caps" due to being stupidly placed and the fact they even can be worn as one. Curbs are "Bottomless Nintendo Pits," like in the Super Mario Brothers games that you have to jump over to proceed further. Litter I see as "Soccer Balls" because I constantly kick them while walking and sometimes hit other people by accident. Bags are "Foot Grabbers" because I always get my feet caught in the bag handles or straps, then stumble or trip around. Electric cords are "Snakes" that like to wrap themselves around my ankles, and they even have two "fangs" at the end. So many obstacles!

Cane training wasn't all fun and games or all about unanswered questions; however, I quickly learned the single one thing that I disliked about the cane. The trainer kept telling me to hold the cane in front of me while I did the swinging. That is a rather painful technique because every time the cane jams into grass, cracks in the sidewalks, sewer grills, and other nooks and crevices, the cane jams right up into my stomach, kidney, or liver area. Imagine that happening a couple times each minute during a travel session. Additionally, my fingers get sore from gripping the cane trying to prevent it from jabbing backwards into me. I had to figure out a way to overcome this.

Obviously the trainer's technique wasn't working, so I elected to ignore it. In the future I will devise my own technique. The solution can be surprisingly simple. I can devise a simple gauntlet wrap, where I could put the hand-held end of the cane inside the gauntlet. It resembles one of the ninja gloves with claws or similar to *Wolverine*, the fictional superhero in the Marvel Comics X-Men team, except there aren't any claws, and the cane is mounted under my wrist rather than the top. My fingers do not have to hold the cane itself, and the cane does not jab into my sensitive areas anymore. Problem solved!

RE-INVENTING THE CANE

With the training complete and the future cane handling issue put aside for later, I got to thinking about this new low tech device.

Surely it must have more uses than just swinging around and whacking people by accident! I decided to look at its potential humorous side. I got to thinking. What could I do with my cane to make the anxiety go away and laugh?

♦ Fishing. Tie a string with bait at the end of the cane and just flick it. No hearing needed to feel the fish tug the line once caught.

♦ Chopping trees. Just add a blade alongside the cane, and you can chop some serious firewood.

♦ Writing. Dip the cane tip in some ink and then get writing.

♦ Riding. Ride the cane like Harry Potter during a Quiddich match or horseback riding with John Wayne.

♦ Picture frame. The cane can be folded and bent in sections to create a spiffy picture frame. Would be great for artistic themes!

♦ Weight Lifting. How about using it for weight lifting the easy way. Arnold Schwarzenegger has nothing on me.

♦ Boat paddle. You could use the cane to paddle your canoe instead of an oar. Best of all, you could take your girl out for a romantic moonlight cruise, and have the light reflect and sparkle off the cane's reflective coating.

♦ Shoveling. It's always nice to help mom with shoveling snow or dirt.

♦ Sports: Baseball. You could hit a ball with the cane and score a home run. Golf. You could play putt-putt with the cane at the mini-golf course, or take a great big swing at the main golf course. Croquet. Just a hard swing with the cane, and the ball hops through the croquet arches. Billiards/pool. Whack the cue ball with the cane and feel the table shake as the balls go flying all over the pool table, scoring into the baskets.

It can be really tough teaching profoundly deaf Usher people cane training and handling. Using humor can certainly take the anxiety out of it. Home states like my own do not have experienced staff to deal with deaf-blind. It can be done if the client and staff are determined enough. Uninformed people say that individuals who have Usher syndrome can't do many things. Ironically, people with Usher can do a lot more with a simple cane than hearing sighted people think.

Cane Power, indeed.

ABOUT THE AUTHOR

Randy DeWitt has Usher syndrome type 1 and lives near Boston, Massachusetts. He earned a B.S. in Digital Imaging and Publishing Technology from Rochester Institute of Technology (New York) and a B.S. in Graphic Design from Northeastern University in Boston. He is currently involved with advocating for Usher syndrome in Massachusetts, and the Usher Syndrome Coalition.

CHAPTER 16

TEN THOUSAND MILES FROM HOME

A CONGENITALLY BLIND STUDENT GRADUATES AND CHOOSES
TO RELOCATE SO AS TO TEACH GEOGRAPHICALLY ISOLATED
USHER 1 PEOPLE ORIENTATION AND MOBILITY SKILLS.

LELAN MILLER

The four weeklong summer cane training class required for all aspiring Orientation and Mobility (O&M) instructors started June 4, 2013, at Texas Tech University. I will always and forever remember the first words the O&M professor said to me as I staggered into her classroom at seven o'clock in the morning that first day, only hours after disembarking from a midnight flight into Lubbock, Texas, population 240,000. The sight of twenty-one new mobility canes and twenty-one new blindfolds waiting for their new owners was startling, bewildering, and unsettling. I wasn't sure if I was supposed to be where I was. "You've come to the right place!" the O&M professor exuberantly greeted me. The journey of ten thousand miles began with those words.

Under her tutelage, my twenty classmates and I learned mobility cane travel under blindfold during the ensuing four weeks. What was blindfold for them was deafblindfold for me because I was the only hearing-impaired student in the class. Under deafblindfold, I whacked the cane back and forth with a "BAM! BAM! BAM!" that always unsettled the O&M professor, who ran flying after me. "Lelan, stop that! We don't hit the cane making so much noise," she said.

"But I don't hear anything or feel anything unless I do that," I replied.

I traveled to street corners and didn't know where and when to cross. The sound of cars whizzing by meant it was not safe to cross; the absence of cars meant all quiet and safe to cross. "Lelan, don't cross until all is quiet," warned the O&M professor.

"But it's always quiet wherever I go," I replied.

We all used a long, straight cane with glide tips. The glide tips were like the tips of classroom chairs used in primary schools, meant to minimize the scraping and grazing of floor wax. It also minimized contact with the tactile world to the barest essentials. We learned the standard two-point touch. Tap here, tap there, tap here, tap there. There was nothing tactile between the two taps. Classmates could hear a great deal of information from the cane's taps. I couldn't. They also could hear a great deal of information from the environment around them. I couldn't.

By mid-June, I secretly doubted the words the O&M professor uttered to me the first day of cane class and was not convinced that I was in the right place. This was getting to be more like the wrong place. It seemed like the long straight cane with the glide tip wasn't designed for the deafblind. The cane traveler had to hear the cane's language. I couldn't hear the cane's language. What was the cane saying to me? Nothing.

I convinced myself that O&M was going to be another failed life endeavor for me, and I was getting ready to drop out of the program when classmates started murmuring about someone coming out from Louisiana to teach street crossings with a mobility cane in a few days. I didn't know anything about Louisiana except that there were a lot of swamps and alligators. I was afraid of what we were going to be doing and didn't think this was going to be a good career choice for me.

The Louisiana mobility instructor came and during the course of the first lecture, he had me demonstrate something. Since I was not following the instructions given, he realized that I wasn't hearing the directions. She said something to him. He whirled around to her and whirled back to me, but this time he looked startled. Judging from his surprise, I guessed that she told him that I couldn't hear. I smirked at his surprise, but said nothing. The next day continued with more lectures and demonstrations. "Lelan, are you listening to him? This is going to be on the test," the O&M professor warned me.

I absently nodded in her direction and then turned to speechread him giving the lecture. Then he signed to me, "This is going to be on the test." He signed? The O&M instructor signs?

He smirked at my surprise, but said nothing. I went into shock. I don't know what anyone else was thinking at the moment, but I couldn't understand why an O&M instructor would know sign language. O&M was supposed to be all about the blind, not about the deaf. In my mind, this was all "blind stuff," so what was the point of knowing sign language? I stumbled out of that class and staggered back to the dorm in dazed shock, though I retained some presence of mind to toss the course-withdrawal form into the trash that night. I was here to stay.

After the course finished for the summer, I went home to wait for the internship assignment. I fully expected to be assigned to a blind rehab center somewhere in Texas, my home and where I lived. Finally, my O&M internship assignment came in the mail. I eagerly tore it open only to discover the unwelcomed news—I was going to Louisiana! I flew into a rage. The internship coordinator at Texas Tech rebuffed my numerous attempts to re-assign me to a site anywhere in Texas with a terse reply every time. "You are going to Louisiana. Report there in June."

No further explanation was provided. I fumed. A nine-week internship was mandatory to become an O&M instructor, and all other internship sites in Texas were already full. I had no other options.

Resigned to fate, I angrily threw my belongings into the car and set off for Louisiana on June 4, 2014, exactly a year after the O&M professor cried out to me, "You've come to the right place!"

Only this time around, I was going to a wrong place called Louisiana. The O&M instructor at Texas Tech who had signed to me, "This is going to be on the test," was going to be my supervisor in Louisiana this summer. The second day of the internship, he sent me a text message: "Meet me at 5 p.m. today in the vending room on the first floor."

When we met, I found out why I was sent there and not to a blind rehab center somewhere in Texas, like most of my classmates. "I asked for you to be assigned here for the internship," he said. "You know sign language; you know deaf culture; that's why I asked for you to come here. We have a large population of deafblind people with Usher syndrome here. Your job for the next nine weeks is to go out to the nursing home and teach them how to get around the area and go outside using the cane. We also have some deafblind folks with Usher living in the community. I want you to go find out where they are and what they need to learn and teach them."

I was speechless. The previous summer I had learned to teach cane travel to the hearing blind. How was I supposed to teach cane travel to the deafblind? They could never hear the language of the cane. This was going to be impossible. "I'm in the wrong place," I darkly thought to myself as I headed off to the nursing home the next day.

They were having their monthly birthday party when I came in and sat at a table. The party room had a celebratory atmosphere complete with cake, balloons, and party favors. However, I was hardly in a celebratory mood myself. Then I went into shock with the realization that nearly all of them were fully deafblind from Usher syndrome type 1. Hands reached out to find out who I was and to tell me who they were. Within moments, flying fingers were conveying to fellow flying fingers that I was the new O&M intern just arrived from Texas. Brows furrowed. Doubt crossed deafblind faces. Heads shook in dismay. Debates and discussions ensued.

Stunned at the sight of so many people with Usher syndrome in one place, I stared and watched in disbelief as deafblind flying fingers flew all over the party room. "Lelan? From Texas? She's deaf? Knows sign? She's teaching what? Teaching O&M? How is she going to do that if she can't hear the tap of the cane?"

"O&M is blind stuff, not deaf stuff. Why is she doing this blind stuff?" they questioned.

Others joined in the debate and argued for the need for O&M

training by signing: "It's not blind stuff– it's deafblind stuff. We need stuff like this."

"Can she teach me some? I went to Louisiana School for the Deaf, then went completely blind after I graduated. I never learned O&M."

"Big Al went to Louisiana School for the Deaf and was blind after he graduated. He never learned O&M. Lelan should show him how to cane from his room to outside."

"Ollie sits in my room all the time, and he won't go anywhere without me. Lelan should teach him how to go to the dining room, outside and the party room, by himself, so he doesn't sit in my room so much. I want some time to myself, and I want my room to myself!"

"Good idea! Tell Lelan."

The discussion went on to include deafblind individuals who did not even reside in the nursing home, but needed O&M training. "Has she ever talked to Bob who lives by himself in the apartment off Johnston Street, about five miles from here? Tell her to find Bob. Teach Bob something."

Someone else added: "Oh...yes. Bob. He keeps asking about how to get to the apartment manager's office and the bus stop and the gym."

"And Jojo, too. Talk to Jojo. She wants to learn O&M for her workplace and her apartment complex." Within minutes I was flooded with endless requests for O&M instruction.

Hours later I staggered back to my dorm ready to submit my resignation note to the O&M supervisor because I didn't know how I was ever going to do this and was ready to give up. All those people with Usher syndrome wanting O&M! This was going to be impossible. It was well after midnight. I passed by the O&M office on the way to my dorm room, the office door left ajar by the night cleaning crew. There was a huge basket full of canes of every type and with every kind of tip in the office. The basket looked like a Thanksgiving cornucopia overflowing with an abundance of various vegetables and harvest grains, except this basket was overflowing with an abundance of canes and cane tips. I called it the "cane-ucopia." The deafblind folks with Usher syndrome I had encountered so far used ball tip folding canes, not the long straight cane with a glide tip that I had been taught to use at Texas Tech. I had no idea where the deafblind around here got their ball tip canes or how I was going to find one for myself and figure out how it worked.

As I reached the office, I stopped in my tracks and suddenly realized the "cane-ucopia" possibly contained the cane I needed to teach O&M to the deafblind. I gasped and scolded myself: "Why didn't you ever think to look there!" Thereupon, I wildly spun around and raced into the office where I raided, pillaged, plundered the cane-ucopia and finally pulled out a ball tip cane the perfect height for me. Ball tip cane in hand, I secretly sped outside into the dark night. I left my Oticon hearing aids in the dorm; the night was my blindfold. In the silent night of deafblindness under the Louisiana sky, I rolled the ball tip to and fro. Unlike the glide tip, which was tapped here and tapped there in a two-point touch, the ball tip rolled all over the landscape.

Rrrrattattarrrattatta, the cane vibrated into my hand. Sidewalk, the cane said to me. Shhhmuussshhhhh, the cane rolled into my hand. Grass, the cane said to me. Pftttthwack, the cane came to a stop with a thud. Brick wall, the cane said to me. Rrrrra-thunk, the cane plunged downward a few inches. Drop off, the cane said to me. Boing boing boing, the cane hollowly thumped into my hand. Empty garbage can, the cane said to me. Bumpa bumpa bumpa, the cane jumped up and down in my hand. Tactile street crossing strip, the cane said to me.

This was the tactile sign language of the cane, the landscape of touch coming into my hands through the cane. The moment was eerily similar to the moment where Ann Sullivan taught Helen Keller her first words with tactile signs. For the first time I was learning and understanding the tactile language of the cane, and the ball tip cane was my Ann Sullivan and I was the Helen Keller.

Eager to cover more and more of this landscape of touch and to discover more and more tactile language of the cane, I recklessly sped up my pace. The cane abruptly stuck into a crack in the sidewalk, bent slightly and then flung me into a freshly planted flowerbed. "Idiot!" the cane said to me as I sprawled through petunias and begonias. The journey of ten thousand miles was building momentum. I tossed the resignation note into the trash. I was here to stay.

The next day Jojo found me in the O&M office. Jojo was in her mid-forties and had Usher syndrome type 1. She was profoundly deaf from birth, and her vision had gradually diminished, vanishing in her mid twenties. She worked upstairs in the iCan Connect office. She was out much of the time training other Usher syndrome deafblind clients how to use iPhones, iPads, and HumanWare technology. Jojo was apparently an important figure in the Louisiana deafblind community and once a month she would convene deafblind meetings in the meeting room in the building beyond the courtyard.

"Can you teach me O&M to go from my office to the meeting room? That's where we have monthly deafblind meetings, but I always have the interpreter walk me there. I want to go there myself," Jojo said. I agreed.

Later that afternoon I went to the nursing home and found Ollie in his brother's room. Ollie was in his late fifties, and, like Jojo, he had Usher syndrome type 1. He had become completely blind soon after he graduated from the Louisiana School for the Deaf. From age five he had been amplified and for decades he had bilateral Oticon hearing aids exactly like mine. His speech and auditory perception was actually quite good. His brother looked tired and annoyed, but he perked up when I popped in. "Hey, you're back," Ollie's brother excitedly waved to me. "I remember you! This is Ollie over there. Can you teach him O&M to go from here to the dining room? And outside to the patio where he can listen to the marching band practice on the football field next door? He is always following me around and he never leaves me alone." I agreed.

Then I went across the hall where Big Al was. Most of Big Al's family had Usher 1. Staff reported to me that Big Al sat in an armchair in his bedroom almost all the time, constantly signing to himself, unless a nurse came to walk him to and from the dining room where he would sip hot coffee until the meal was served. He seemed to be in a world of his own. Someone said everyone had been trying for years to get him to move on his own but nothing worked. I decided to try to do something about it.

Later that day I went to visit Bob in his apartment complex five miles away. He eagerly signed his specific request for training to me: "Someone told me the soda vending machines are next to the apartment manager's office, and that's where I pay the monthly rent. Usually I have my next-door neighbor take my rent there. I've got a cane. Do you have time this summer to show me how to get there and back? So then I can buy myself a soda whenever I want, bring my rent check there, and maybe find out a little more about where I live." I agreed. I would soon learn that Bob was a prominent respected member of the deafblind community in Louisiana, and he would often "talk" with me for endless hours about the deafblind culture, the prevalence of Usher syndrome in Louisiana, and the importance of tactile communication. He especially stressed what to do and not to do when teaching O&M to the deafblind.

The next nine weeks of teaching the tactile language of the cane and the landscape of touch were absolutely magical. Everyone learned so fast, and they amazed me to no end. Those who had Usher 1 taught me almost everything I was supposed to know about teaching O&M to the deafblind–things I never could have learned anywhere in Texas. No other place in the world was as magical as Louisiana in the summer of 2014. I could not imagine myself anywhere else. Even hearing of my fellow O&M interns' glowing reports of their internships in Texas was of absolutely no interest to me whatsoever. They were all working with the hearing blind.

By mid-summer, the journey of ten thousand miles was charging forward with exponential speed. Jojo learned to walk from her upstairs office down to the first floor, then go out across the courtyard and to the meeting room where she conducted meetings. Ollie learned the layout of the entire facility and could travel to any point within the grounds. By summer's end he was traveling with the cane out to the patio where he would enjoy hearing the pounding percussion and blaring brass of the high school marching band practice a few yards away. Big Al was a struggle, but in the end, all I had to do was sign into his flying fingers "Time for sunshine." He would then retrieve the cane, unfold it, and stroll outside. Bob discovered, to his delight, that his apartment complex not only had a soda machine and an apartment manager's office, but also had a bus stop and a convenience store just steps away from his front door. He met staff and residents he had never before met. Time with them was absolutely magical as I witnessed more and more deafblind flying fingers take flight with canes.

The summer was coming to a close, and I found myself fighting a rising tide of fear and dread of my eventual return to Texas. Most O&M interns left at the end of nine weeks with a celebratory sense of homecoming, but by August I was fighting a rising tide of nausea within me that always accompanied dread and despair. Texas was not home to me anymore. My life in Texas was meaningless until the moment I arrived in Louisiana, the land of deafblind flying fingers that emerged from everywhere into my palms wanting O&M. And at the end of the summer, there were still so many deafblind flying fingers wanting to take flight with canes, but I had no choice but to return to Texas where I had no sense of belonging and no niche in life. I was going to leave my home of always and forever, where I had a sense of belonging, where I was totally at home among deafblind folks with Usher syndrome.

The journey from Louisiana back to my so-called home in Texas felt and seemed like ten thousand miles, so great was the agony of leaving. The late August sun cast melancholy shadows that laid long and low across the Louisiana land as if to tell me my journey of ten thousand miles was now coming to an end. With each and every mile marker along the highways taking me thousands of mental miles away from my home of the summer of 2014, the O&M professor's first words echoed in my mind again and again: "You've come to the right place!" Yes, I was in the right place. I was at home, my home of always and forever.

ABOUT THE AUTHOR

Lelan Miller resides in Texas and has had Congenital Rubella syndrome from birth. She holds a Masters degree in Deaf Education from Illinois State University and trained in Orientation and Mobility (O&M) at Texas Tech University. Lelan completed the O&M internship at Affiliated Blind of Louisiana in the summer of 2014 and is a certified O&M instructor. She is now teaching O&M to those who are deafblind throughout Texas and Louisiana.

CHAPTER 17

INDEPENDENCE DAY

EVER CURIOUS, THE AUNT OF AN USHER 1 MAN TRIES HER
HAND AS A DEAFBLIND PERSON WITH A WHITE CANE ON THE
4TH OF JULY TO SHOW THE OBSTACLES AND OFTEN IMPOSSIBLE
ACCESSIBILITY ISSUES PRESENT IN THE CITY OF BOSTON. THE
HURRICANE WAS EXTRA.

CHARLOTTE J. DEWITT

In an inspired moment of bravado, someone you know decided to go undercover and pretend to be blind, white cane and all, at Boston's annual July 4th celebration, moved to July 3rd due to Hurricane Arthur. I had to be nuts! But I really wanted to experience what an Usher 1 person would encounter attending an outdoor public event with nearly 100,000 people cheering fireworks at Boston's Esplanade park along the Charles River.

That was the low side of estimated attendance, Beach Boys and all, as normally on July 4th, there are 600,000 to 1 million people listening to an outdoor Boston Symphony "Pops" concert at the Hatch Shell, picnicking, and revving up for the traditional finale: a performance of the *1812 Overture* (Boston's summer equivalent of Handel's *Messiah* at Christmas) and fireworks. Arthur, however, had a few things to say about that, and the authorities listened, shortening the concert by eliminating the *1812*, and shortening the fireworks just in time, as within 15 minutes, the heavens opened up with no warning, and pounding rain drenched everyone just as they evacuated the park.

Now I suppose that's OK for most people—it was, after all, nearly 80F—but the question remains, with myself as the undercover blind person—how many hands does a deaf/legally blind

Usher syndrome person have, especially one with advanced RP (*retinitis pigmentosa*, or tunnel vision, for the layman)? If you are deaf and can't see at night, how do you simultaneously hold a white cane, hold the shoulder or arm of a friend for guidance, hold an umbrella, and sign? And if your friend doesn't know sign language, how do you write your communication, hold a flashlight so you can see the page, and juggle your white cane and umbrella, all at the same time? And that's if a car doesn't hit you as you're trying to cross the street.

But I digress, as there was, with foresight, a flashlight, just not one that I could manipulate while I ambulated (or should I say stumbled) with my white cane (and cheating, as I could see, even though I pretended I could not). Oh, and I forgot—my solution to the umbrella situation was that I brought a couple of bags from the dry cleaners– an easy solution for a poncho, which I didn't own, light-weight, actually perfect– as long as it didn't cover your nose and mouth while you were breathing. That could have been nasty. But it still didn't prevent me from having to wade across flash-flooded streets.

Boston's quaint cobblestones are uncompromisingly challenging to a white cane user. Just as you think you're getting the hang of swinging that cane in an arc in front of you, left/right, left/right, sweeping the sidewalk clear, leading the *Charge of the Light Brigade* going down Clarendon Street towards the Charles River and The Esplanade park, WHONK! Your outstretched arm is propelled into your gut because that stupid little red ball at the end of the cane has encountered an immoveable object: an irregular cobblestone victimized by frost heaves during the Ice Age.

Then there was the incident where (I confess, it was deliberate) I allowed the cane to go between the legs of a 20-something-year-old young lady who wasn't paying attention to my *Pilgrim's Progress* and cut in front of me. She apologized profusely.

But I forget—in this exercise, I am also supposed to be an undercover deaf person (an older Usher 1 victim without a cochlear implant) who is also legally blind. So technically, I should not have heard her apology. Actually, I wouldn't have heard the Beach Boys either, but that is another story.

My pride would not let me put a sign on my back (sort of like "Danger: heavy load" that you see on the gravel trucks). I naïvely thought the white cane should have been enough of a concession. Well, that's OK, but only during the day. At night, everyone else is as blind as I am. What white cane? But then, they can hear, and that gives them a decided advantage.

That brings me to switch hats and assume my real life alter ego: that of a public events producer on the scale of the finale of Singapore's Millennium Chinese New Year's celebration.

In spite of the fact that this was the 41st July 4th celebration on Boston's Esplanade, in spite of the fact that America has been celebrating Independence Day since 1776, in spite of the fact that people today profess to be super-sensitive to the special needs of disabled people, in spite of all this, I (the illegal deafblind person) heard or read of absolutely nothing concerning provisions for people with "my" (or any) disability. It begs the question: Is the burden of discovery all on the person who is deaf and blind, or is there a moral obligation for public officials to ensure the safety and well-being of all people attending a public event, especially an annual event (not a one-off) of this magnitude?

Frankly, from the perspective of my new alter ego, I was shocked.

I am coming to realize that as intelligent as a deafblind person may be, as motivated, as schooled in such things as mobility training with a white cane, sign language, tactile signing, lip reading, etc., our society—the world's society—is not set up to allow a deafblind person to be fully independent, no matter how much the person wants his independence.

If you have vision problems, for example, Boston's Back Bay underground train station platform is a dungeon. The only notice of an approaching train is the vibration of the platform as the train approaches. There are no electronic signs saying "Providence: Track 1." There is only a garbled loud speaker announcement which hearing people even have difficulty understanding. If the track changes from track 1 to track 3, the only announcement at the platform level is an audio announcement. The good news is that there is a wide yellow "bubbled" strip just prior to where you would fall over onto the tracks. Except that if you are blind, it is only your feet that will notice this, hopefully in time.

In my fantasy identity, I have a genius level IQ. I have graduated from two universities, a total of nine years of full-time academic programs. I WANT to be independent.

Unless something changes in our society, I don't see it happening.

Happy Independence Day.

ABOUT THE AUTHOR

Charlotte DeWitt is the proud aunt of an inspirational Usher 1 person and a member of the steering committee which produced this book. She also served on the planning committee for the 2014 *International Symposium on Usher Syndrome & Usher Syndrome Family Conference* that took place at Harvard Medical School in Boston, Massachusetts.

In her other life, she is a member of the International Festivals and Events Association (IFEA) *Hall of Fame*, the industry's highest honor. As president of International Events, Ltd., she has served as a cultural ambassador and events architect and strategist in some 30 countries since 1979. A Certified Festival and Events Executive, Charlotte is founder/past President/CEO of IFEA Europe and lived in Sweden from 1994-2004. Her book *Culture Smart! Sweden* is now in its fifth printing.

PART 4

PROFESSIONAL LIFE
AS AN USHER PERSON

CHAPTER 18

WHEN ONE DOOR CLOSES

A TEACHER OF ENGLISH AS A SECOND LANGUAGE REPATRIATES
AFTER AN OVERSEAS POSTING AND RE-INVENTS HERSELF AS AN
EXHIBITOR IN ARTS AND CRAFTS SHOWS IN AMERICA.

AMY BOVAIRD

"I'm on my way. Be ready."

Ready? I'd been waiting for the past half hour. I touched the raised bump dot that helped me locate my cell phone receiver button and tapped it off. It wouldn't be long until my younger brother arrived. I pressed my face up to the garage door window, squinting, finding the blurry view even darker than normal. Though still August, the air that morning was cool enough for my breath to fog up the window pane. Rain splattered and slid down the glass outside. A steady stream of water gurgled through the gutters. "Rain, rain, go away—"

"B-beep!" Don's white pick-up pulled into the driveway. I found the small round button on the front wall beam and held it down with my finger. The garage door shook and rattled to life, the motor groaning with age as the rusty wheels moved the door in starts and stops until it came to a final shuddering halt. I let go of the button.

My brother backed in and emerged from the driver's seat. He eyed my many containers. "Think you're going to sell all this, huh?"

"Yep." I stood to one side with my white cane as my brother loaded the cardboard boxes into the cab. He leaned over again. "Sorry, this is gonna get soaked in the back of the truck. Hope it's waterproof."

I wondered what he meant by "this." But when I heard him complain about how heavy it was, I knew he meant the two wooden drawers that held my books and the cross-stitched Palestinian pillows I'd picked up from my travels. With his foot, he tapped the plastic bin that housed the rest of my crafts, then lifted it over the side of the truck. "This board goes, too?"

Board? I paused. Oh, the whiteboard. I thought he meant some plywood. "Yes, that, too."

Don pulled out, and I made sure the garage door was securely shut. My pink baseball cap in hand, I swiftly pushed it onto my head, wishing I had a hooded raincoat that wouldn't flatten my hair. "I'm going for it," I yelled, wondering why I wasted my breath. His window was closed. I swept my white cane back and forth through a puddle and tried to shield my face from the rain with my free hand.

Don slid across the seat and opened my door. "Hop in!"

I sluiced the water off my cane and folded it in two before sitting down. The door clicked shut, and the hum of the engine cut off any conversation we might have had. His windshield wipers ran full speed as he backed out of the driveway and we headed to the shop to pick up his rustic furniture.

We would sell our wares at a local church. I cast an anxious glance at the lead-colored sky when we arrived and grimaced as I sought to identify the entrance. The weather outside always affected the lighting inside a place. "People are pretty helpful about giving directions," I mumbled to myself.

My brother carried my boxes in and set up a table for me. I only had to wipe down my containers, unload my crafts, and list my prices. "You're a good guy," I told him.

"Yeah, well, someone's gotta do it," he said, wandering off.

I took a paper towel and as I dried the drawers, felt the newly bubbled veneer of the wood under my fingertips. I slid a drawer open and pulled out a book. No problem there. The furniture was a casualty of the rain. I started unpacking the boxes.

The lady from the adjoining table said, "Can I help you?" I accepted. Maybe she'd have some ideas of how to make my display look more appealing. She emptied something out of a plastic bag. "What's this bracelet thingy made of? Looks like some kind of paper bead."

I wasn't sure which one she meant. "Oh, the bracelets." I was happy to explain. "I'm the middle man for a Filipino Livelihood Program. There are a couple kinds of bracelets." I picked one up. "This one is in the shape of a fish." I outlined it with my finger. "And when you put it this way, it looks like round bread." I said, poking it in another direction. "I sell it and send the money back to the Philippines. My college friend from 'way back heads the non-profit group."

"Neat." The woman chatted with me as we arranged my table together.

Even though I could have done it myself, it was a nice way to get to know her, and it was thoughtful of her to help—considering she didn't know the extent of what I could or couldn't see. I picked up the whiteboard and sat down with my marker, hoping people could read my writing. It was getting more difficult to write in a straight line these days since I couldn't see the letters clearly.

When I finished, I leaned the board up against my table. I spied her nametag. "Mar-Marge, what are you selling?"

"Take a look." She covered her mouth with her hand. "I mean—"

I smiled to put her at ease. No biggie. At the front of her table, I leaned in and hoped I didn't look too weird as I scrunched up my face to see better. Terry cloth. Were they tea towels? I moved closer, my nose almost touching a soft pile. I patted it.

The woman must have been observing me because she said, "Tea cozies. Two sizes. I made them all myself."

Tea cozies. I'd never have guessed. Toaster covers, I might know.

The sale started, and we sat in silence waiting for customers to notice our wonderful goods. People trickled past. Finally, out of boredom, I picked up my white cane and decided to go for a walk to see what the other vendors were selling.

What was that pretty cloth? Was it embroidered? When I

reached over to feel the texture, a woman snatched it out from under my hand. "That's mine!"

"Oh, sorry." I quickly moved to the next table. As I hesitantly worked my way around the room with my cane, one table drew my eye. Reds, pinks, greens were all lit up. Gorgeous colors. But, what was it? The bigger shapes had one color. As I moved closer, I saw they were lamps. The smaller pieces twinkled in several colors. Necklaces? No, they were flatter. Boxes? I pointed. "What … um?"

"This night light is $5.99," the man said, assuming I was asking the price.

"I'll be back soon," I promised as I moved on. I returned to my own table to wait. And wait. Finally, I had a buyer. She left with a fish bracelet. By lunchtime, I'd given out exactly one business card and hadn't sold a single one of the devotional anthologies that included stories I'd been so proud of.

The afternoon was only slightly better. The church had more vendors than buyers so, to kill time, we traded with each other. I bought a lovely night light before settling back down and trying to sell again.

My table covering contained a color-coded map of Africa so it generated occasional conversations about travel. One lady asked me if I had traveled to South America. I said I'd lived in Colombia.

"I lived for several years in Paraguay," she said and launched on a long, drawn out explanation of missionary work.

When I could finally get a word in edgewise, I said, "I met some people on the coast of Paraguay."

"On the coast? Do you mean Uruguay?"

I struggled to format the map of South America in my mind. "Um—"

"You must, dear," the woman said smugly, "Paraguay is a land-locked country."

"Yeah, that's what I meant. Paraguay and Uruguay are next to each other," I added to regain some credibility after a thirty-year gap of travel in that part of the world.

"They are *nowhere* near each other." The woman spoke with some asperity. "I should know. I lived there sixteen years."

La-dee-dah! So much for my travel expertise.

Around two o'clock, I decided to make my way over to the restroom. I grabbed my white cane and set out. The farther away I walked from the selling area, the darker the area became. *Yet I was certain the restroom was on this side of the building.* I slowed down, tentatively slid my cane back and forth a couple of times over the polished floor and paused.

"You lookin' for somethin'? Can I help ya?"

I smiled in the general direction of the male voice. "Yes, thanks! Just trying to find the bathroom." The tip of my white cane was forward, seeking some kind of crack an inch over the floor or along the wall.

"The bathroom door's right there," the person said. "Can't miss it."

"Thanks!" I said, taking the voice literally. I leaned over and pushed *there*. Nothing happened. I pushed again. Harder. The door didn't give way at all. Finally, I realized that I was pushing against the wall.

I giggled. "Oops! I won't get very far trying to open a brick wall," I chided myself out loud, controlling the urge to look back and see how many people had witnessed my blunder.

Just pretend you have no idea that happened. Keep going.

My hands moved to the left. I groped. Finally, I felt a thin lever: *the door handle.* Still chuckling, I turned it and disappeared into the restroom. Inside, I took a deep breath. I must have looked like a mime with my hands moving over the wall like that. Only instead of wearing white make-up, I wore a bright red face.

Inside the restroom, I had the normal challenges of finding where everything was, the most difficult being the soap dispenser and the knobs to turn on the water. I also had to figure out whether there was an air blower or paper dispenser, and if there was the latter, where the trash receptacle was located. Not an easy feat.

Finally, I exited the restroom. I shielded my eyes and bit my thumbnail, unsure where to go next. My heart beat faster. *I hate this. How do I get so turned around*, I asked myself, wringing my hands together. Someone with what looked like a clipboard walked past me and I called out, "Trying to orient myself here. Where is the vendors' circle of tables?"

"At the end of this hallway, it opens up to an auditorium. The vendors are there."

I took a deep breath and thought, I can find this. No problem. By following the hallway out, I found the auditorium. There, I looked for the light shades stall, which I remembered was near the hallway. I moved steadily across the room. When I heard my brother's voice, "Stop. You're back," I knew I'd reached my table. I folded my cane neatly and placed it under the table.

That afternoon, with few customers to distract me, I had time to think. It frustrated me when someone who obviously saw me navigating with my cane gave me such vague directions. Where actually was "there?" To the right? To the left? Straight ahead on a brick? No wonder I was having difficulty finding it for myself. I was so ready to take all the responsibility ... or the blame ... for my mistake—when it was actually someone else's lack of awareness.

To be fair, maybe that person didn't see my white cane. Perhaps he was intent on what he was doing himself and just heard my question and responded automatically. I couldn't count on everyone being detail-oriented. I recalled my gaff with the location of Paraguay and the woman's smugness. I didn't want to make anyone feel silly. But this wasn't the first time this had happened. I went into problem-solving mode.

Negotiating directions in a strange place was a dual effort. I guess I needed to say, "I'm visually impaired. Can you help me find the bathroom door?" If they heard those words, it would remind them that I couldn't see "there" and needed specific directions. If that didn't work, I should have asked for concrete directions. Or maybe asked him to walk me to the bathroom door, although that might have felt weird since he was a man.

But sitting there at my table that day with all my unsold books and crafts, I found the humor in my situation. The old adage "When one door closes, another one opens" popped into my head. That day I added my own personal twist to it, "Or maybe, one isn't even a door at all!"

ABOUT THE AUTHOR

Amy L. Bovaird comes from northwest Pennsylvania, not far from beautiful Presque Isle on Lake Erie. She suffers from Usher syndrome type 3. Currently, her hearing loss overshadows her vision loss.

Amy graduated with a B.A. in Teaching English as a Foreign Language and an M.A. in Bicultural/Bilingual Studies, which she earned from the University of Texas at San Antonio (UTSA). She also garnered an honors certificate in CELTA (Cambridge English Language Teaching to Adults). For 17 years, she taught English as a Second Language overseas, dividing her time between South America, the Far East, and the Middle East. When she returned to the United States, she thought she had stepped into a foreign country.

She recently published her memoir, *Mobility Matters: Stepping Out in Faith*, a humorous, faith-based book about coming to terms with vision and hearing loss. Amy chronicles her adventures with a completely blind mobility instructor. She is a speaker who uses humor, faith, and great passion to share her journey with her audience. Read more of Amy's adventures at www.amybovaird.com.

CHAPTER 19

MY USHER'S LIFE LESSONS

A SUCCESSFUL ATTORNEY ADAPTS, WITH HUMOR, TO A NEW LIFE.

MARY DIGNAN

I remember how I wanted to die, or at least for the Earth to open up and swallow me forever, when I read that memo telling me how I'd been asking questions that had already been asked and answered, and how I'd said things that were irrelevant and inappropriate at our meeting earlier that day. I had always known that the hearing problem was more of an issue than the visual field loss associated with Usher syndrome. Now, this memo was the proof that I never should have tried being a lawyer, that I had no business in this profession and should just go home.

Instead of going home, I got up to close the door to my office, sat back down at my desk, and picked up the memo from Tom to read it again. Tom was my supervising attorney, and we had both been looking forward to that meeting with a potential new client. The work would be on an issue that no one at the firm knew better than I, and we were sure we'd close the meeting with the retainer agreement in hand.

But the meeting just didn't go well. It started off well enough, but there were some odd pauses in the conversation, moments of uncertainty and careful courtesy, and I didn't feel good about it when it was over, even though we did, in fact, end up with the retainer agreement. I was still thinking about the meeting a couple hours later when Tom's secretary came into my office and handed me an envelope, sealed and marked "confidential."

It was a memo from Tom. "Mary, I need to make you aware of some things I observed during our meeting today." He listed specific things I'd said and described how I'd asked questions that had just been discussed, and how I'd said things that were irrelevant to the actual conversation. He said he and the client both knew I wore hearing aids and assumed I simply hadn't heard things accurately. He said that because I had an excellent reputation as a truly competent professional, and because he and the client knew how well I knew the issue, they had made allowances for me, and we got the account. Still, Tom was concerned. "Mary, I'm wondering if you're not hearing as well as you used to, and if there is anything we can do to help."

My hands were trembling as I put the memo back down on my desk, and I felt a hot flush rise up from my toes to my face. God, what an incompetent idiot I must have sounded like. I was even more embarrassed by the courteous smiles and patient repetitions, the polite allowances they had made for the incompetent idiot. It would have been better if someone had just growled at me to go put in some fresh hearing aid batteries.

But, when I read the memo yet again, I began to appreciate the inherent respect and sincere consideration Tom was showing me. Instead of confronting me with the painful truth, Tom could have just stopped working with me. He could have started whispering behind my back: "Uh, best not give that assignment to Mary– she can't handle it." Or, "No, Mary's not the best one to attend that meeting– she can't handle it well." And I would have slipped into miserable mediocrity.

He didn't and instead, he came to me and told me exactly how I wasn't cutting it and gave me the chance to find a way to measure up. I decided that before I handed in my resignation letter, I'd at least find out if there was a better hearing aid out there. I called my audiologist and told him what had happened. He told me I was already using the best and most powerful hearing aids available, but there might be one other thing I could do. "It's time for you to get an FM system. Come on down this afternoon and we'll get you set up." This was an assistive hearing device that would enhance the use of hearing aids and therefore, allow me to hear better.

I was in my early 40s then, down to less than 5 degrees of tunnel vision and wearing two high-power hearing aids. I still had good precision vision within my little tunnel. For the last twenty years of slow but steady vision and hearing losses, I had always figured out ways to work harder and smarter. It was the hearing losses that troubled me most. I'd been wearing the best high-power hearing aids for years and was so good at reading lips and body language that it was easy to forget I had a hearing problem. But as my vision started to go and I could no longer read lips and body language well, we all began to comprehend just how deaf I really was. It didn't matter so much that I was mowing down my colleagues in our office hallways, but responding inappropriately to clients and judges was a huge problem.

It took practice and patience to develop the skill to use my new FM system effectively, but the effort paid off. My FM system worked well because I made it work, and I made it comfortable for everyone around me to work with me.

There were several lessons, or rather reminders, for me out of that whole incident, including the fact that it's just about impossible to die of humiliation, no matter how much you may want to. More importantly, I was reminded that everyone around me took their cues from me—if I was uncomfortable with the fact that I had to use an FM system to hear, everyone else would be uncomfortable with it, too. So I not only learned to use the FM system well, I also learned to introduce myself and my tools with candor and humor.

"Hi, I'm Mary Dignan from Kronick, Moskovitz, Tiedemann, and Girard, representing the State Water Contractors, and that's my FM system in the middle of the table there. It helps me hear, and I would appreciate it if you would not touch the mike or the wires because it sends a lot of irritating static directly to my hearing aids." I'd pull my aids slightly out from behind my ears to make them obvious, and then I'd put them back and go on. "The other thing you need to know about me is that I only see through a little keyhole," and here I would make a keyhole tunnel of my fist and peek through it, "which means I can see you." Then I would point at someone else, "But I don't see Tom sitting next to you," and pointing at Tom, I would continue, "This is a good thing because I don't like looking at Tom anyway."

That would generate a few chuckles. "This is my cane," I would add, picking up my telescoping white cane from the table and opening it. "I use this to find the stuff that doesn't show up in my keyhole when I'm walking around, and it's also highly useful for whacking people in the ankles and *patooties* (editor's note: contemporary American euphemism for rear end)." More chuckles, and then we'd move on and get down to business.

I learned not to waste energy on trying to cover up my vision and hearing challenges. That meant I had more energy to focus on doing my job, and doing it well. I didn't worry about attending conferences or night meetings, because I learned how to use my white cane to get around on my own safely and gracefully. I also learned to ask for and accept a helping arm with grace. I learned that if you are good at your work, and especially if you are a good team player, your colleagues will be willing to make any reasonable accommodations you need. Even before the Americans with Disabilities Act (ADA) and the term "reasonable accommodation" joined our vocabulary, I had no problem getting hearing aid compatible phones, lighting and other low-vision aids, adaptive computer technologies, and even cab rides when I had to stop driving.

I learned that when my colleagues knew I was putting my best effort into making things work, most of them were willing to put in a little extra effort themselves to help me out. Sometimes it was as simple as giving me an extra few seconds to get my FM system set up before they started the meeting, or steering me around pillars, potted plants, and people that always seem to get in one's way at a crowded conference, or giving me a ride home. Sometimes it was sending me a memo telling me honestly about some problems I needed to be aware of in order to figure out ways to solve them.

The FM system was a good solution for a few years. It turned out that, apart from Usher syndrome, one of the reasons I kept losing more of my hearing was an acoustic neuroma brain tumor that grew out of the cochlear nerve to my right ear. The surgery to remove the tumor saved my life but exacerbated my hearing and vision challenges so much that I had to give up my legal career.

Ten years after the brain tumor surgery I received a cochlear implant, which greatly improved my hearing. I still have trouble with background noise, and I can only hear out of one ear, but I hear better than I ever could before. It is the one thing in my life that has gotten easier. I am 60 now, with almost no vision left except some high-contrast shapes in a world of murky shadows spiked with glare.

Those lessons I learned years ago still apply today, and I have come to realize that this is because they are Life Lessons, not merely issues particular to Usher syndrome or any other disability. I have also come to realize that part of learning and developing one's abilities is as much a lesson of disability as it is ability. One such lesson came from my friend Brian, an extraordinarily competent computer wizard who was born blind.

Brian can listen the way I used to be able to read a thousand words a minute, and his orientation and mobility skills are awesome. We often talked about the differences between being totally blind from birth and going blind later in life. Apart from the life adaptation and grieving issues, the main differences we noted involved the ways we perceived and comprehended the world around us. I told him about a totally blind guy who had a hard time wrapping his mind around the concept of transparency. He just couldn't make out how a hard cold pane of glass that he could rap his knuckles on was something you could "see" through.

"Oh, I don't have a problem with that concept," Brian said. "My problem is pictures."

"Pictures?" I questioned.

"Yeah, pictures," Brian said. "How can you put a three-dimensional world onto a flat piece of paper?"

I remember my jaw dropping as I stared at him and began to comprehend how rich and real the world is to Brian. He can't see any of it, but he knows it intimately. He moves in a world that he perceives physically and kinesthetically through all his other senses. He is always aware of how his surroundings feel, smell, and sound. In a lot of ways, he is much more aware of and intimate with his world than most sighted people who superficially see their worlds from a distance and from a flat piece of paper.

Brian taught me that even though I am losing all my sight, I still have a rich world to perceive through touch, taste, sound, feeling, smell, and experience. This, too, is a Life Lesson, not just an Usher thing, but it is a lesson sweeter because of Usher syndrome. It does not lessen the pain of losing my vision, and it doesn't even necessarily make my life easier. But it does give me hope and joy. It is the reason I'm still doing my mosaics (with a little sighted help here and there), the reason I'm still in my kitchen baking from scratch and making up new recipes, the reason I can tell when I'm on the beach or in the redwood forest, or even just out on my patio enjoying the evening breeze and garden scents. And it is the reason I know I still have a good life to live.

ABOUT THE AUTHOR

Mary Dignan was diagnosed as mentally retarded before the moderate-severe deafness was diagnosed close to age five. She was then fitted with hearing aids and attended public schools. At the age of 20 she was diagnosed with *retinitis pigmentosa* and years later, was told she had Usher syndrome type 2.

Ms. Dignan earned a B.A. in English/written communication from Santa Clara (California) University in 1976. Her twenty-one year career in agriculture and water resources management issues includes work as a news reporter, legislative aide to the U.S. House of Representatives in Washington, D.C., and the California State Assembly Committee on Agriculture in Sacramento, California. She earned her *juris* doctorate with distinction from the University of the Pacific, McGeorge School of Law (California) in 1994 and practiced law until 1997. She now creates and teaches mosaic art, and her work has been shown in several public venues including Sacramento Society for the Blind and the Canadian Helen Keller Centre in Toronto, Canada. Her community service includes serving on the Sacramento Board of Supervisors' Disability Advisory Committee and on the Board of Directors of the FFB (Foundation Fighting Blindness), Sacramento Chapter. She is a present member of the Sacramento

Embarcadero Lions Club. Ms. Dignan lives in Sacramento with her husband Andy Rosten.

CHAPTER 20

REDEFINING INDEPENDENCE AND EMPOWERMENT

THE AUTHOR REFLECTS ON THE 9,280 DAYS SINCE SHE WAS
FIRST DIAGNOSED WITH USHER SYNDROME, HER CAREER AS A
SCHOOL PSYCHOLOGIST, AND THE PIVOTAL MOMENT OF GIVING
UP HER DRIVER'S LICENSE.

ROBERTA GIORDANO

Today is June 27, 2015, and it has been 9,280 days since I was first diagnosed with Usher syndrome. That was over 25 years ago. I was an 18-year-old freshman in college and had already been living with a severe-to-profound hearing loss since birth. Of course, there were challenges growing up with hearing loss, but I knew how to do that; it was all I'd ever done. Now as a young adult just starting out on my own, experiencing college life and making decisions that would shape my entire future, the diagnosis was Usher syndrome (*retinitis pigmentosa* and hearing loss). What on earth were these big words? I'm going to go blind? On top of deafness? Seriously, how does an 18-year-old process this information?

I will tell you it has not been easy; there were times when I just wanted to curl up in a ball and hide from the world in the safety and comfort of home, where I didn't have to work so hard just to hear, just to see. I did exactly that, hide from the world, from time to time over these past 25 years, but I'm proud to say that I spent far more of my time doing whatever I had to do to achieve my goals and live life out there in the world. It's been a journey every step of the way and sometimes living with Usher syndrome is an exhausting journey, but it's one I've learned to embrace with more positivity as I've gotten older.

In fact, if you had told me four years ago that this journey would take such a positive turn based on the pivotal moment of surrendering my driver's license, I would have thought you were crazy. Now it has been 1,450 days since I stopped driving, on my 40th birthday, because *retinitis pigmentosa* stole away too much of my peripheral vision. Yet, surprisingly, these past four years have taught me volumes about feeling empowered rather than disabled, feeling grateful rather than self-pity, and feeling hopeful rather than bleak.

It seems that so many of the significant milestones of my journey have been concentrated within these last four years since I had to stop driving. But of course, as with all of our journeys, I must start at the beginning. When I was a newborn, my parents had just learned that my older sister had a significant and progressive hearing loss. She was three years old. By the time I was thirteen months, my parents were able to get a confirmed diagnosis for me, and I began wearing hearing aids shortly thereafter.

One of the most important life lessons I learned from my parents throughout my childhood was that being hearing impaired did not mean lowering our expectations; it just meant modifying them so I could reach my goals in a different way. Little did we know at that time how often I would have to modify my expectations and adapt my approach toward reaching my goals, because living with progressive hearing and vision loss meant frequently having to figure out new ways to get things done, even the smallest, most routine tasks in everyday life.

During my childhood, my parents made the decision for me to be educated in a traditional public school environment, being fully mainstreamed with hearing peers while also being supported by a teacher of the deaf. I was an academically strong student, I loved learning, and I don't recall feeling at any major disadvantage in the classroom due to my hearing impairment. I graduated from high school with much success and had the honor of being accepted for early admission to my first-choice college, Tufts University, near Boston.

It was in January of my freshman year at Tufts that I went to Massachusetts Eye and Ear Infirmary (MEEI) in Boston to have my eyes evaluated, on the recommendation of my ophthalmologist. He had noticed some unusual pigmentation in my retina, and even though I was not having any symptoms, he knew there were possible correlations between hearing loss and eye issues. I don't recall his ever putting a name to this, though. At MEEI that cold January day, my parents waited around for hours and hours while I was subjected to an extensive battery of tests, and that was the day we heard about *retinitis pigmentosa* and Usher syndrome for the first time. I was going to lose my vision, progressively. There was no way to predict how much vision I would lose or how fast I would lose it. The doctor told me that I could be totally blind in my 20s or 30s or perhaps not until I was in my 80s. There was no way to know and very little to do to stop it.

The doctor entered me into one of his clinical studies, which lasted the next six years and required me to have all these eye tests every year to track the progression of my loss. I remember when the study concluded and I received in the mail a printout of all of my "numbers" from the test results each year. I scrutinized those numbers over and over, feeling overwhelmed by the changes, the decline from year to year, and my numbers as compared to the norms. By this time, I had graduated from Tufts and was trying to decide what was next in my life. I knew I wanted to go to graduate school, but I did not know what career path was right for me. It took me two years after college to motivate myself toward a new goal, and I think I was terrified to pick a graduate program and career path, not knowing if and when the blindness would come.

I honestly don't recall how I proceeded in making the decision about graduate school and career path. I think I had just reached a point where I knew I had to do something more than the clerical work I did for two years post-college. So I bit the bullet and applied to graduate school programs to begin my training to become a school psychologist. I figured I might be good at working with children with disabilities because I had my own disabilities. I also thought that working in an educational setting might offer me added "protections" if and when I needed accommodations for my disabilities.

I completed a three-year program at the University of Massachusetts, Amherst, earning a Masters in Education and a Certificate of Advanced Graduate Study (CAGS) in School Psychology. I was excited to do my internship year at Clarke School for the Deaf in Northampton, Massachusetts, a residential school for deaf children who communicated orally (as opposed to using sign language). For the first time in my life, I was in a setting surrounded by people just like me! It was both a comfort and a learning experience.

Once I got my credentials as a school psychologist, it was time to venture forth in the world yet again, but I wasn't quite ready to leave the comfort of my experience at Clarke. I was able to work as a psychology research assistant at nearby Smith College for a year while also doing consulting work at Clarke. After that, it was time for me to get my official career as a school psychologist underway.

I will admit, I lacked confidence and was so sure that nobody would want to hire me, just in general, but also because of my hearing impairment. At that point, my vision was still a non-issue, relatively speaking. After many job interviews, I was finally hired, and in September 1999, I was truly starting my career. I have absolutely loved being a school psychologist ever since. Just last week was the end of my sixteenth school year in my profession!

My journey dealing with Usher syndrome has been ever-present over these sixteen years on the job, though sometimes more than others. The honest truth is that prior to losing my driver's license four years ago, I was usually forthcoming only about my hearing impairment, both in my professional life and in my personal life. Any mishaps I had due to poor peripheral vision and night vision, I did whatever I could to "fake it," which usually meant pretending that I was just clumsy when I tripped over something or absent-minded when I didn't notice someone trying to get my attention beyond my restricted field of vision. As far as I was concerned, if I was doing my job well, and I was, then I had to keep my vision issues hidden from as many people as possible. It was stressful and exhausting, I had frequent headaches, and I sometimes spent entire weekends "recovering" from the stress of my job. I knew that Usher syndrome was taking a toll on me but I was stubbornly determined not to admit it, not to reveal it.

That worked for many years, at least on the professional front. I did not ask for or need any accommodations, other than strategically placing myself in a good seat during meetings. Eventually, I had to start asking for some accommodations at work. I began using an FM system during my one-to-one testing of students to ensure I was better able to hear what they were saying. I also was issued a larger-screened laptop to make it easier to see while I was writing reports. I was lucky to have a boss who had become a good friend, so that made it easier to ask for what I needed. She helped me realize that asking for such things was not a sign of weakness, but rather this support would enable me to continue being competent in my job. This very much lines up with that important life lesson my parents had taught me as a child, to not lower my expectations but to adapt them so I can still meet my goals.

Then came time for me to renew my driver's license, and I just knew my time as a driver was up. I had already spent many, many years terrified of the day I would have to stop driving. How can a 40-year-old single woman have a life if she can't drive? I had already limited my driving to daytime only, which meant never being the designated driver among my friends and always being the first to leave a social event if I had driven, in order to get home before dark. Losing my license altogether meant a total loss of independence, in my opinion. It meant I couldn't "fake it" anymore and would have to come out to the world as a visually impaired person.

I shed a lot of tears in the weeks leading up to that trip to the DMV (Department of Motor Vehicles), knowing I would have to take the peripheral vision test on that stupid machine. The DMV agent asked me what color the square was. What square? I couldn't see it, couldn't even find it when I frantically scanned and searched, my eyes darting back and forth. I leaned back and told the agent I wouldn't be able to see it, but she insisted I try again, that the square was just off to the side of the viewer box. Nope, it's not there, I checked and checked again. Nothing but darkness. My heart was pounding out of my chest, I broke into a sweat, and I could feel the tears building up as she gave me the form to take to an eye doctor for a full eye exam. This was it. Even with a full eye exam, my peripheral vision had reduced to 40 degrees. Not quite legally blind, but reduced enough to disqualify me from driving in the state of Massachusetts, which required at least 120 degrees of peripheral vision.

To this day, I still don't know what color the square was in that DMV machine. Instead, on the day before my 40th birthday, I went back to the DMV to have my photo taken for a State ID card. I felt sick to my stomach that day, but I insisted on driving to the DMV, knowing it would be my last drive. My father came along for the ride, and he drove me home afterwards. This event, while emotionally devastating, ended up being one of the most positive turning points in my life and in my journey with Usher syndrome.

After that day, I began figuring out how to hire drivers, ask friends for help, and learning that I would have to say no to attending social events if my friends or a hired driver couldn't take me. For work, it meant coordinating a new schedule between buildings because I could no longer do mid-day switches from building to building as a district-wide employee. From that day forward, I was officially "out" as a non-driver and a visually impaired person. Over the next four years, there would be many logistical difficulties, disappointments, and feelings of being a burden to others. But let me tell you, I never would have expected all the positive blessings that have come to me as a result of this transition. My friends only proved to be as support-ive and valued as I always knew them to be, but now it is sim-ply undeniable, and every day I ask myself how I got so lucky to deserve these friends. They go out of their way, sometimes way, way out of their way to get me and bring me back to their homes—in different states even! And then bring me back to my home the next day! My colleagues do the same for work drives, from time to time, when one of my hired drivers is unavailable. Even the process of hiring drivers, though at times frustrating, has turned into the blessings of meeting several real "gems" in this world—women who are just happy to be helpful to me, for a fair price, but I always joke that they will not be getting rich off of me! That was okay with them because they have generous souls. These are people I would never have come into contact with had it not been for my Usher syndrome and having to give up driving.

Another blessing that has come over these past four years since I stopped driving is that my family has truly rallied together in talking more openly about having Usher syndrome. My sister was diagnosed much later than I was. While I learned at age eighteen, she did not know until she was forty. Together, we took some empowering steps into the world as a family coping with Usher syndrome. My parents and I attended our first Family Conference of the Usher Syndrome Coalition just the day after I stopped driving, and I even spoke as a panelist at the conference to share my story.

My sister created a Facebook page called *Usher Me In* to raise awareness and share her experiences with Usher syndrome. She even asked me to be her co-administrator of the page so that we could both share our experiences. This served as a way to bring us closer because we were talking so honestly about our daily experiences and frustrations. We had not realized we had so many common feelings because we just hadn't really talked about it before. All of a sudden, she and I had each other as that someone who just "gets it."

The thing about Usher syndrome is that the impact can be felt during the big events in life but almost more importantly, during the really small, daily events, events most people don't even process in their minds. A family member leaves their shoes on the floor or leaves a cabinet door open. These are a big deal to us when we don't see them in our peripheral vision and trip over the shoes and whack our head on the cabinet. Such mishaps can and often do trigger major emotional reactions: anger, frustration, sadness, grief. Other people are not expected to understand this because our reactions seem so out of proportion to the event. For us, it brings back every other mishap, every other time we felt embarrassed or angry because of Usher syndrome. And it brings up all the emotions we know we will experience again and again and again as our vision continues to deteriorate. So finally, with my family now being more open about Usher syndrome, we found support in each other, common knowledge we didn't even realize we shared, and some comfort in knowing we will continue to walk this path together, especially when the cycles of grief come around again.

For me, dealing with the vision loss has been more of an adjustment than the hearing loss, simply because being hearing impaired is all I've known since birth. Just when I would get used to a new loss of vision, it would happen again and even though it was gradual, the changes in vision meant almost constantly dealing with the grief of a loss.

Three years ago, I began to notice a much more drastic change in my visual acuity. All these years, I had prided myself on retaining correctable central vision quite close to 20/20, but in the course of just months in 2012, I noticed my central vision failing me. The small cataracts I had always had were quite suddenly having a significant functional impact on my central vision. I couldn't see the computer screen at work, I couldn't see the print of the test protocols that practically defined my job, and the glare of any white paper or screen was practically nauseating. I struggled to lip read my colleagues just four feet across from me at conference room tables.

Tests confirmed my visual acuity had deteriorated from 20/20 to 20/200 and 20/400 in a matter of four months. Once again, my boss was able to accommodate me with keyboard stickers with bold letters and color contrast I could see and with a simple software tool, a screen reader, to enlarge text and reduce glare on my laptop. I had to photocopy and enlarge test protocols after seeking permission from the test publishers. Personally, I felt like my world was going blurry, I was walking more slowly and awkwardly, and I couldn't communicate with my loved ones across the room because my lip reading skills to aid my hearing were suddenly unusable when I couldn't see their lips.

After much research and consultation, I decided to have cataract surgery, despite the potential risks with RP patients already dealing with such fragile retinas. Taking this risk and having an extraordinary outcome, visual acuity back to 20/20 for distance, literally felt like a life-saver for me. I was in awe at being able to read posters on the walls, street signs, my test protocols in original print, the closed captions on the television. I could once again use my excellent lip reading skills to enhance my hearing. I knew then that the loss of central vision on top of my restricted peripheral vision had given me a glimpse into the world of blindness like I had never experienced before. It was scary and every day now, I wake up so grateful that my central vision could be restored with cataract surgery. This experience also gave a sense of urgency about all the ways I needed to prepare for what may someday be a more permanent loss of vision.

During all of this time over the past four years, I found a tremendous source of support in a Facebook group for women with vision impairment, and through these connections, I have learned about coping with vision loss, different adaptive technologies for the blind, the training process and emotional journey of becoming a cane user and guide dog user, and much more. I admit, I am still not ready to take these steps toward cane and guide dog use, and I believe it is not necessary at this point in my life. But I have found priceless the exposure to the process and how so many women have taken the journey, overcome the adversity, the anxiety, and the shame, and have discovered a world of increased independence and empowerment. In my own way, in my own world, I have discovered my own sense of empowerment, something I never would have predicted years ago about myself.

Around the same time that my vision was taking a nosedive from the cataracts, I learned that my hearing loss had also gotten worse. I always felt that I did so well with my two hearing aids, yet my audiologist had been trying for years to encourage me to consider a cochlear implant. My answer to her was always, simply but emphatically, no. This time around, though, I realized I had my future to think about. With my vision causing such trouble with my functioning at work, I was faced with the reality that I had to do everything and anything possible to prolong my ability to work in my chosen profession. This included the risks of cataract surgery and now the risks of losing any residual hearing I had in one ear with a cochlear implant. So 2013 ended up being my year of three surgeries: cataract surgery in one eye in February, cochlear implant surgery in one ear in June, and cataract surgery in the other eye in November.

Friends, colleagues, and family were telling me I was brave and inspirational, but I didn't see it that way. I saw these surgeries as taking steps to survive as a fully functional, independent, single, professional woman. I almost felt that I had no choice. Yet again, the decision to get a cochlear implant led me to meeting many people who had already taken that journey, both in person and through several Facebook support groups. I even ventured out to blog about my cochlear implant journey on a new Facebook page I created. This allowed me to document my experiences and feelings, much like a diary but in a public forum that enlightened others and gave me a phenomenal "cheerleading squad" to help me through the often-exhausting and frustrating rehabilitation process.

The cochlear implant was a smart decision, and I've been told that my speech improved, which is always a good thing from a professional standpoint. I also found many aspects of my job to be easier. With a cochlear implant, I could hear high-frequency sounds I had never heard before in my life. Some of this was just annoying but most of it meant that I could have more confidence in my ability to hear the students I tested and hear my colleagues and parents at meetings with greater ease and less dependency on lip reading.

My journey is far from over, and I know I will probably have more obstacles, challenges and frustrations to face as my hearing and vision continue to worsen. I hope I'm old and gray before this happens, but this continues to be the great unknown in my life. I have done what I can, what makes sense so far, to prepare and to keep myself as functional as possible. I am prepared for the fact that there will probably be more steps I'll have to take to sustain this functionality. I will not pretend that this doesn't scare me– it does! It terrifies me, and sometimes it immobilizes me. But I am taking faith in the patterns I've already set for myself, that I can get through this and I can succeed in spite of this. It may take me longer, I may shed a lot of tears along the way, but I have so many good people in my corner, and I think that I will be okay. Usher syndrome does not own me or define me, but I have somehow managed to make it a positive part of who I am and learned how to be confident and empowered because of it. I never would have guessed this to be so when that doctor told 18-year-old me that I had Usher syndrome.

ABOUT THE AUTHOR

Roberta Giordano was diagnosed with hearing loss as an infant and with *retinitis pigmentosa* as a young adult. Later it was genetically confirmed as Usher syndrome type 2C. She has worn hearing aids her entire life until 2013, when she became "bi-modal" with a hearing aid in one ear and a cochlear implant in the other ear.

Roberta earned her B.A. from Tufts University near Boston, Massachusetts, then her Masters degree in Education and a Certificate of Advanced Graduate Study (CAGS) in School Psychology from the University of Massachusetts, Amherst. For the past sixteen years she has worked as a school psychologist.

She blogs periodically about her experiences with Usher syndrome on two Facebook pages: *Usher Me In* (www.facebook.com/ushermein), a page she co-administers with her sister Andrea, who also has Usher syndrome; and *Roberta's Cochlear Implant Journey* (www.facebook.com/robertascochlearimplantjourney). Her community service includes participating in and raising funds for the local FFB (Foundation Fighting Blindness)Vision-Walk.

Currently, Roberta lives in the suburbs west of Boston, enjoys spending time with her friends and family, continues to enjoy playing tennis despite her reduced visual field, and shares her home with her beloved pets Bailey and Gypsy.

CHAPTER 21

AN ODYSSEY THROUGH USHER

AN IT PROFESSIONAL MOVES OVERSEAS AND SHOWS HOW
ACCESS TO TRANSPORTATION IS THE KEY TO PROFESSIONAL
ADVANCEMENT.

MANI IYER

Do not go gentle into that good night.
Rage, rage against the dying of the light.
—Dylan Thomas in *Do not go gentle into that good night.*

One balmy afternoon I had to take my friend to the Philadelphia International Airport, about twenty miles from where I lived in southern New Jersey. The windshield on my Dodge Colt was tinted to help me in glaring situations. I was anxious about the drive, but it was on the weekend, and I did not have any excuse to back out of my offer. My friend offered to drive one way, and I accepted without any hesitation. We chatted along the way, which made time fly, until we arrive at the curbside where he disembarked and thanked me. Anxiety began creeping into me, and I calmed myself by deciding I was going to drive very slowly and ignore all the resultant honking, sticking to one lane and one lane only (I was clumsy at changing lanes), and most importantly, focus on the view ahead only. My self-advice paid off, and I was actually enjoying the drive until it turned dark.

Why did it turn dark so suddenly? Was it some kind of eclipse? Then it struck me that I had entered a tunnel. My heart began racing, and sweat flowed freely down my face. I turned on my lights and muttering a prayer, I decided to slow down to five or ten mph. I decided to focus on the taillights of the cars in front of me. Fortunately, the car ahead did have its lights on. I was ready to slam on the brakes if I lost any sight of the car ahead. It felt like a lifetime before I saw the light of the day at the end of the tunnel. As soon as I got out of the dark tunnel, I decided to break a rule and stop on the shoulder to collect myself. I parked, rolled down the window, took deep breaths, and let my heart beat normally and my eyes adjust before venturing out to merge and continue on with my journey.

Two years later, I was diagnosed with Usher syndrome, at the age of twenty-eight, the result of a routine visit to an ophthalmologist who, failing to give me 20/20 vision with my glasses, suggested I see a retina specialist. A battery of tests at the Scheie Eye Institute in Philadelphia, Pennsylvania, confirmed I had Usher syndrome type 2. Even though I was legally allowed to drive, my retina specialist suggested I stop driving immediately. All he had to say to convince me was that I could strike a child running across in front of my car. My son was one year old then. Now, why did it take so long for the diagnosis despite all the warning signs since childhood?

THE EARLY YEARS: UNDIAGNOSED USHER IN INDIA

I was born in Bombay (now Mumbai), India, to a lower-middle-class family. My father was often unemployed and because of that, we sometimes lived on the fringes of poverty. When I was only sixteen days old, I had a massive seizure. My parents had almost given up on my survival, and the doctors attending me asked them and all family friends to resort to prayer. They prayed, and I miraculously recovered.

I was a fast learner and had mastered the English alphabet and was able to recite all the nursery rhymes by the age of two! My parents were eager to put me in school, and I ended up in kindergarten at the age of three. Little did they know what was in store for me.

My eldest sister had a visual impairment and was hard of hearing, too. Because of her condition, everyone in my house spoke loudly and clearly. There was never a whisper in the house! As a result of this, my hearing loss went unnoticed until my first-grade teacher came to our home to tell my parents that something was wrong with my hearing. Neither the family doctor nor the ear, nose, and throat specialist had any idea what was wrong with me, and, in retrospect, I wonder why did they not even connect my sister's condition to mine? Anyway, arrangements were made at the school for me to sit as close to the teacher as possible, and this continued throughout my academic life. Unbeknownst to me, it was the dawn of my lip-reading talent.

In elementary school I did not show any signs of precociousness and managed to scrape by year after year. My parents forgave me for my poor performance, and this was reinforced by my teachers, who confirmed that I would do very well if only I could hear better. In middle school, it was a different story. I began to shine academically—my brother still jokes about this new development, attributing it to the tightening of some screws in my head. All hearing issues were soon forgotten, and I continued to excel and ended up being the valedictorian of my class.

THE "BUMP" PHASE

Around ninth grade, I noticed that I could not play in the dark with the other kids. It was also the beginning of the "bump" phase of my life. The good old family doctor diagnosed it as night-blindness and prescribed heavy does of Vitamin A. It was also during the same year that I got a taste of hearing aids for the first time. Mine was the boxy kind that you put in your pocket, and it had a long wire running from the box to my left ear. I hated it almost immediately because it produced more noise than sound. I remember the device catching the fancy of my class and teachers who wanted to try it on. Throughout my academic life I was fortunate to be guided by supportive teachers and my parents' love and encouragement. My academic success gave me the self-confidence to face the many obstacles that never seemed to stop, always lurking around.

COLLEGE AND THE WORKING WORLD

Continuing my wonderful, sheltered academic ride with my undergraduate and postgraduate studies in computer science, I was suddenly faced with my first hard reality—my first job as a software engineer in downtown Bombay. This entailed traveling in a train with passengers packed liked sardines and walking on busy streets to catch a bus. Since I had what appeared to be normal vision during the day, I managed it pretty well, albeit a few bumps and shoves, which went largely unnoticed in a perennially crowded Bombay, although I get the shivers when I think about it now. The biggest issue I faced was to ensure that I either went home before dark or, in case I had to work late hours, which was often, to make arrangements to reach home safely. This would often mean having a friend take me home or having my father or brother wait at the train station to walk me home. It was frustrating because anxiety played havoc with me every working day of my life in Bombay, and I was only in my early twenties, dating my college sweetheart and supposedly in the prime of my life.

At the university, I wrote poetry, the romantic sort, and this paid off in getting a wonderful lass interested in me. She would become my wife and my best friend. When we were dating, she knew about my hearing issues and my night-blindness. An Usher syndrome diagnosis was still nowhere near the horizon. I wonder sometimes what course my life would have taken if I had known early on about the diagnosis. Would I have done so well in my academics? Would my sweetheart have agreed to marry me? Would I possess the same zest for life? Would I have led a relatively happy life?

FROM INDIA TO AMERICA

After working for three years in Bombay, I had the opportunity to come to the United States to work as a software consultant for a company in Clearwater, Florida, that manufactured automated printed circuit boards (PCBs). I struggled with my hearing and understanding the American accents, and lip-reading did not get me any further. The project manager bluntly told me I needed to get hearing aids, and that was a blessing in disguise.

I bought my first pair of in-the-ear hearing aids at the age of twenty-five. I still remember the day I walked out of the audiologist's office after being fitted with the new aids. I heard the sound of traffic for the first time, and I couldn't believe my ears. It was an emotional revelation when I first heard the birds and the wind. I actually ended up doing so well in the project that the company offered me a job after six months, which I turned down because I was dearly missing my sweetheart!

I returned to India, but I was "bitten" by the American bug and wanted to return to the United States! After looking for other opportunities, I found a job in Nicosia, Cyprus, and the company promised to put me on a project in Washington, DC. I accepted the offer and this time, I made plans to get married. I flew to Cyprus alone after the engagement, the marriage, and the honeymoon, but the plan was to bring my wife to America once I settled down. Six months later my wife and I were re-united in Washington, DC, and we settled permanently in America.

DIAGNOSIS

Two years later in New Jersey, where I was working as a senior software engineer for a company specializing in software for the police and fire departments, I was diagnosed with Usher syndrome. Despite the diagnosis, I ventured to buy my first house in the town of Marlton. This town had no public transportation, and I relied on rides from my wife or office colleagues, and even the boss's wife. This was overly frustrating since I had to figure out the pick-ups and drop-offs every evening for the next day!

Besides, I was traveling a lot to different police departments in the country, which was another affair laden with anxiety. But the police officers were some of the nicest people I met in the country. They picked me up at the airport, dropped me off at my hotel, and left special instructions at the desk for them to keep me safe in case of evacuations. And in the evenings, the officers entertained me before taking me back to the hotel. Before any consulting "gig," my boss had to ensure that I was taken care of, and all my special needs met. This alleviated some of my anxiety, but the feeling of dependence gnawed at me again and again.

LIFE AS AN USHER FATHER

A few years later, my daughter was born. I noticed that my frequent travels were taking too much time from my growing kids, and I was worried they would begin to think they were raised by a single mother! I decided to move to a city with adequate public transportation. I had worked as a consultant to a mutual fund company in Boston, and I approached them for a permanent position. They were more than happy to hire me, and thus began a new phase of my life. My wife had to give up her job, my two children were uprooted from their familiar settings, and I had to figure out my new transportation route. It required a bus and two subways to get to my place of employment. I still had pretty good central vision on which to rely, and I quickly learned the new ropes.

Along with the loss of night vision, my peripheral vision was slowly diminishing over the years. During my student years, I would often stumble over anything in my path. My family would chastise me for not looking where I was going while walking. They blamed it on me being an absent-minded genius. I remember my brother constantly hitting me on the head and scolding me when we walked together. It was fun being with him, but I paid a heavy price and had to be on high alert at all times. While working in Bombay, I was tripping people in front of me, unable to step into a moving train or bus. (That is how the young and stupid boarded trains and buses in India, and I was no different.)

After a few years, my wife found a job in a suburban Massachusetts town, and this necessitated a move because she had to be the one in charge of the day care and school for the kids, since I no longer drove. I was thrilled to find a suburb that had four train stations, and we decided to buy a house and settle down. I had to take just one commuter rail to get to work. It was a forty-five minute ride, and I used it to read the newspaper or a book and snooze on the way home. I could not have asked for anything better. My wife was happy with her commute, the kids loved the new school and were beginning to make new friends, and I was in the groove. I also found a great counselor from the deafblind unit of the Massachusetts Commission for the Blind, a great retina specialist, and was making new friends in the Usher community.

TRANSITIONS

As luck would have it, there were rumors of the company getting bought out and hence, moving elsewhere. It was the internet boom period, and I decided to try my luck in the gold rush before the inevitable happened. I did find a job at a startup company that promised to conduct all projects in-house. There was a hitch though—there was no public transportation available to the new employment location. The para-transit service came to my rescue.

Things were starting to look good—I was learning a lot of new technologies related to the internet and was enjoying the vibrant energy of a startup. A year later, I sensed that the company was in trouble, with multiple layoffs and talks of sending consultants on projects requiring travel and a long stay away from home. I got into action, started looking around again, and found a job next door. One such time, I walked into the company with my resumé and got an interview and the job in a few weeks. I was off to greener pastures.

It was while working in this new company that I noticed that my central vision was slowly failing, and I increasingly had difficulties in accomplishing some of the routine tasks in software engineering. The VP of the company also noticed my bumping into people and things. My heart froze when he called me over to his office one day. He insisted that I start using the white cane and said that the company would support me in whatever I needed to do to move around and do my job. He also added that he had an ulterior motive and wanted other employees to see me with a white cane. Hopefully, this would inspire them to be more productive! It was an emotional day for me because I was just not ready for a white cane.

After much convincing from family, friends, my counselor, and the nice woman from the Human Relations department, I arranged for mobility and orientation lessons. Soon after, there was an ergonomic evaluation of my workplace and low-vision aids. Things were happening too fast. Every transition was difficult both emotionally and functionally, requiring constant adaptation and more adaptation before I settled down with a given set of parameters. I had to grit my teeth and move on. I began to work longer hours, taking work home just to catch up with my own load. My vision had slowed me down considerably, and I was not yet ready to accept this fact

USHER AND EMPLOYMENT

After a relatively long period in this job, I decided to move to yet another employer due to an inconsiderate new manager and my desire to seek fresher pastures. This time I made up my mind to work for a well-established company and simply stay put. I found a great company that was very supportive of my disability and did not think any differently seeing me with a white cane in my many interviews with them. It was back to more mobility and orientation lessons, more low vision training, ergonomic evaluations, and the whole nine yards. My central vision was fading at a faster pace, and I was finding it more and more difficult to accomplish my once routine tasks and was relying on my colleagues. This was getting increasingly frustrating, and I became depressed in the evenings.

The company believed in a "meeting" culture, and my hearing wasn't helpful there. I used the FM system but it necessitated a discipline among my colleagues to talk to one person at a time. My managers tried to enforce that rule, but it was soon broken. In addition, I had to give PowerPoint presentations in dark meeting rooms (ambience for the sighted), and I found myself getting out of sync with the slides that I could not see.

In three years, my vision plummeted to a new low, which prompted me to start thinking of throwing in the towel. I started talking with a disability lawyer, the HR folks of the company, and my manager. After months of agonizing deliberations with many people, I quit. I had worked for nearly thirty years in the software engineering field, and it was now time to think of other alternatives, to re-invent myself, as one friend put it.

GOING GLOBAL: THE USHER SYNDROME COALITION REGISTRY

Long before the Usher Syndrome Coalition was founded, I met Mark Dunning, now the Coalition's Chairman of the Board, through a common acquaintance. I told him my story and offered my services as a volunteer for whatever idea he came across. Together, we brainstormed and concluded that a global registry for the Usher syndrome community was the first step. He encouraged me to start working on developing the registry, and after two years of painstaking work, all alone in a room, the Usher Registry was launched in April of 2013. Today the registry is translated into many languages and boasts a membership of 850+ individuals from 40 countries.

THE BLIND ODYSSEY

Meanwhile, I was also contributing poems on a regular basis to the *Vision through Words* blog (www.visionthroughwords.com)

run by Stella DeGenova, a visually impaired artist. Through Stella, I heard of a poetry fellowship from the National Endowment for the Arts (NEA) for visually impaired creative writers. I applied for it and won a one-month residency fellowship at the Vermont Studio Center in Johnson, Vermont. It was there that a lot of peer poets and writers convinced me that I had talent for poetry and that I should pursue a Master of Fine Arts in Poetry.

After I returned from Vermont, I started contacting the admissions departments of several universities offering the MFA. I applied to several and got into one close to home. At the time of this writing, I have finished one year of the MFA program and believe me, it was a difficult year. Now I understand why kids complain of homework! I am missing out on the visual aspects and the music of poetry. But, nevertheless, I enjoy writing poems, and words and lines are constantly buzzing in my head.

So far, it has been a great journey, despite all the travails, and I have been extremely fortunate to come across some of the nicest people who have encouraged and supported me from my childhood to present day. Where will my blind odyssey take me next? I do not know, but I continue to have dreams that include publishing a book or two of my poems, pursuing a doctorate in poetry, mentoring kids, and helping the underprivileged. With all modesty, I would like to end with a snippet from one of my poems:

He walks into many a wall.
He makes many a false step.
He is as human as any.
He is as divine as none.

ABOUT THE AUTHOR

Mani G. Iyer was born and raised in Bombay (now Mumbai), India, and was diagnosed with Usher syndrome type 2 at the age of twenty-eight. He attended St. Xavier's High School and earned his undergraduate degree in statistics and a Masters Degree in computer science from the University of Bombay. After finishing his graduate studies, he worked in Bombay as a programmer/analyst for two years before coming to America to work as a software consultant. He has lived in the United States since then and was a software engineer for about twenty-seven years in Florida, Washington, DC, Virginia, New Jersey, and Massachusetts.

Mani currently lives in Needham, a suburb of Boston, with his wife, two grown children, and a beautiful pet West Highland white terrier. He has very little useful vision left and is severely deaf. He loves listening to audio books, jazz, and of course, writing poetry.

Mani volunteers for the Usher Syndrome Coalition and developed the Usher Registry. He is also pursuing an MFA degree in creative writing (poetry) at Lesley University, Cambridge, Massachusetts.

CHAPTER 22

STEPPING STONES

AFTER INTENSIVE MOBILITY TRAINING WEARING BLINDERS TO
LEARN SELF-CONFIDENCE USING A WHITE CANE, A BRAVE
YOUNG WOMAN MOVES TO CHINA TO TEACH IN AN
ORPHANAGE.

AUDREY CHARD

The best and most beautiful things in the world cannot be seen or even touched—they must be felt with the heart.
—Helen Keller

Sitting in a dark, cold office waiting for the doctor to come in to give me either good or bad news, I just stared at the floor waiting and waiting. The door opened and I froze, not knowing what to think or say. The doctor's words floated around me as I tried not to hear her. I believe her words were, "Audrey, we have some bad news. You have *retinitis pigmentosa* as part of Usher syndrome, and you are going blind. We recommend that you don't drive anymore." I had just heard not one, but two heart-wrenching pieces of news, and my world fell apart around me. The world as I knew it, my life as I knew it, was about to change.

I had finally come to terms with the fact that my hearing impairment was a part of me. I was diagnosed with moderate hearing loss at the age of two and started wearing hearing aids then. It was difficult to accept it because most of my childhood I was bullied for my speech, my hearing aids, the FM system I wore, and more. I had anger already inside me from the challenges that it brought upon my life. I did extra homework and speech therapy so that I could be in the grade with my age group. It was enough just dealing with being hearing impaired, and now I was also going blind. I thought I was going to break.

I was three months from high school graduation, and I had just bought myself a 1986 Volkswagen Cabriolet convertible. The thought of not being able to drive anymore—I just couldn't put it into words. The sense of independence I felt as I drove down the highway with the windows rolled down, the wind blowing my hair, and the music blaring was an escape from reality for me. The independence of being able to drive wherever I wanted and not having to wait or rely on others was such a great feeling. But being told you should not drive any more– it is so much harder and so different from how you would feel if you yourself had chosen not to do something anymore. When it is taken from your grasp, it is like a piece of yourself is taken. You no longer feel whole.

I was coming to a wrap on my softball career after going to the Babe Ruth World Series two years in a row as a left-handed pitcher. I had played for 10 years, playing on traveling teams, a city league, and in high school. I was asked one year to join a traveling team in Gig Harbor, Washington, to join them in a tournament in Colorado. It was an honor to be asked and noticed for my skills as a pitcher. The diamond was where I shined. It was there that my confidence was built. Not being able to be on that pitcher's mound in control, I didn't know where I could find my confidence again. I felt lost and angry.

I had to start from scratch once again. It was like a huge corn maze, and I'm still trying to find the end today, an end where I would be feeling full of confidence along with a sense of new independence within myself. Every dead end becomes an obstacle that I have to battle with in order to get back that piece of me that was taken. After being diagnosed with Usher syndrome, I changed. I felt alone and became shy, scared, quiet, depressed, bitter, insecure, and angry. I had to start somewhere, regardless of how I felt.

My first stepping stone was attending the Washington State School for the Blind (WSSB) for a program called Learning Independence for Today and Tomorrow (LIFTT) after graduation from high school. I went in blind, so to speak, because I had no idea what to expect. I was introduced to a wide variety of vision impairment and blindness disorders. I no longer felt alone, and I considered myself one of the lucky ones. I had a chance to see the beauty of nature, faces of loved ones, sunsets, and had a chance to play softball. I learned a lot of skills including how to live on my own with others with vision impairment, orientation and mobility, how to ride the city transit, how to read braille, and how to manage my personal finances. It was quite an experience and it made me realize that I had to find myself through what I could still do, rather than focus on what I had lost and could no longer do. Easier said than done, yes, but it was progress. Being in the program showed me that with training and patience, I could find that confidence and a different way of independence. My type of independence is no longer hopping in the driver's seat, but rather taking the city transit, a taxi, or walking.

I was no longer able to play softball, but I found another sport that I could do– paddling. I joined Blind Ambition, a Dragon Boat team that consisted of 70 percent vision impaired or blind paddlers. It was amazing! Paddling started to give me back a sense of confidence. I was one of the stronger paddlers needed in the front of the boat to get the jump at the start line. The excitement and adrenaline that runs through the team members as they paddle hard, while the coach yells and beats on a drum for the team to paddle to, so that everyone keeps the same rhythm, is astounding. Some people may not be able to picture how blind people can do this sport, but it simple. The team members paddle to the beat of the drum and when it quickens its time, they know to speed up. If the team falls out of sync, the paddle is pulled out, and the paddling starts again into the rhythm. There is no vision needed for this sport. All one needs to do is listen to the beat and feel the paddle. Finding a place to fit in and being good at it gave me a sense of confidence again.

I started volunteering through WSSB after school programs. I taught a girl who was completely blind to snow ski for the first time. That feeling of seeing her smile and filled with joy made a spark light up inside of me. I kept volunteering as much as I could to help the students. I knew what I needed to do was to keep feeling this sense of satisfaction helping others. My volunteer work lead me to my next stepping stone and the greatest life experience ever.

I had the opportunity to go China to volunteer at an orphanage for vision impaired and blind children for two months. I was in charge of writing lesson plans, and teaching arts and crafts, cooking, and sports. I also helped teaching English. It put life into perspective, and I realized how lucky many of us are and how easy it is to take things for granted. All these kids were full of smiles, laughter, and love, even though they were dropped on a doorstep, and some had been abused. All they wanted was to be loved and have a family. I wanted to bring them all home with me, especially one little girl who became my shadow from the day I arrived. This experience helped me find myself and by doing that, it helped release some of that anger and bitterness I had building up inside of me. These children showed me that I should be grateful for what I have, and that I need to focus on the positive and the future of my life. No more thinking of the past.

After my time at WSSB I settled down in Port Angeles, Washington, my hometown, and bought an old craftsman's cottage. Port Angeles is a small town, and it was hard to find people to accommodate my limitations. I was certified as a medical assistant but was not able to get a job because of my vision problem. I became a medical office assistant instead and worked the front office of a very busy doctor's office and the call center. I felt that since I was not able to be a medical assistant, I had to prove to myself and to my boss that I could still do a great job regardless of my peripheral vision loss. I went above and beyond by training others, creating procedure manuals, and taking on extra work. In the end, I became a valuable employee and a trainer.

Ten years after my diagnosis, I took another huge step by moving away from the comfort of my small town to attend the Idaho Commission for the Blind's program called Assessment and Training Center (ATC). I lived in the dorms, and this was where life started to look up. This program was more intense and educational than what I did at WSSB. I had a class schedule, and all day long I had to wear black shades, which made me look like a bumblebee,. The purpose of the shades was to train the brain to use other senses and not rely on vision. The shades plus the training prepared me the best I could be for that time in the future when I may have no vision. It was emotionally and physically draining experience, but worth it.

In the class designed to cover activities of daily living, I learned how to cook on an electric and a gas stove, baking, chopping; how to pour liquids, measuring; and how to set up the table eating area at a restaurant, to use a BBQ grill, and to do laundry and sewing. I learned to use the sense of smell and touch in cooking. You can smell the difference in a hamburger or the feel of eggs to know when they are done. This class proved to me that I don't need to have help cooking or doing laundry as long as I label things correctly and I am cautious. I cooked my first fried egg and flipped it perfectly! These little things made me do a happy dance. The biggest challenge was using the BBQ grill, which was not what I expected. When I was flipping the chicken, it would feel like I had found the next piece, but it wasn't really a different piece. I ended up flipping the same ones over and over or stacking them on top of each other. Let's just say that it was bad enough that my teacher thought she should inform me, but at least nothing fell through the cracks!

Orientation and Mobility (O&M) tends to be a class that builds confidence and independence. It is very scary, and I will not sugarcoat it. There are days that I want to deny that I need to use the white cane and I end up making a fool of myself by body slamming someone, running into a pole, or something along those lines. O&M taught me to navigate downtown Boise under shades. I would have to remind myself to take deep breaths and breathe. I would get headaches from straining to hear the traffic or the different sounds the white cane makes to let me know if I'm in a driveway or a sidewalk. Most days I wanted to throw my cane or rip the shades off, but I knew that it wouldn't help. My hearing impairment made mobility with shades harder, especially when it was raining or snowing. I had no problem toughing it out because I knew that my instructor was following me and would save me from any danger.

My last assignment was finding Java Café on my own. I made it, but with difficulties because it was raining. I had to peek twice after being stuck in two different areas because of the water drainage pipes. I couldn't hear the traffic over the noise. My instructor was proud of me for accepting the challenge, knowing it would be tough. Even though it was a struggle and it will continue to be more difficult as my vision worsens, I am comfortable, and the white cane is now an extension of my arm. However, I am scared to think of when and if the time comes that I have no vision. I know that I will be too scared to go out on my own, so I will need to relearn mobility to get the independence back again. I can't give up.

The other classes I took were braille, computer, and woodshop. Yes, you read correctly, woodshop under shades! Woodshop was my favorite class. When you close your eyes and picture yourself using an arm saw or table saw, it is scary. Actually doing it is another story. You are taught safety first and how to position yourself when using each machine. When I turn the arm saw on, I am so focused on my hand placement and holding the piece of wood securely that I don't notice the sound it makes. Even though I am not in tune to the sound the saw makes, when it makes a sound that it shouldn't make, I notice it. I know that I did something wrong or I need to make adjustments when that happens. This class gave me the most confidence boost. It allowed me to come out of my comfort zone and try something I never thought I would be able to do. It allowed me to design my own project and build it. It was a huge accomplishment to see a finished project that I thought I could never do or picture it in my mind completed. "Never" was not a word used in this training facility. If you can work a machine, you can do anything you put your mind to. It is possible to do woodshop with no vision. I am proof, and I still have all my fingers!

The classes were not the only places where I learned things

that helped me– dorm life was an adventure. I made two friends who helped and supported me. We pushed and believed in each other. We had different types of vision impairment, but that didn't matter. We were all going through something similar, the same frustrations and fears. Training was so tough and mentally draining for us that we had to find an escape after facing our disability all day. We would go on adventures and be goofy while using the white cane. Laughter was our medicine. Dorm life helped me come to accept my disability more because we could relate and express how we felt inside. The support that they gave me helped me grow stronger. One night when we were walking home from dinner I turned around and said, "We look like a cane gang with all of us walking with our canes." "Cane gang" stuck, and it became our group name.

Confidence and independence don't happen overnight. It has been eleven years since my diagnosis, and I'm still working on it. I have days that are tough, but doesn't everyone have them? I am at a better place now, and I know that if I push myself and have patience, I can do it. These experiences helped me find myself again. They helped me find the confidence that leads to finding my own independence. It made me not want to feel trapped with no way of getting around on my own. I need to live in a place where I can be free to walk anywhere without feeling unsafe and to be near bus routes. I don't want to have to rely on family or friends to drive me all the time.

As the visual field loss progresses, I know that with training and support from family and friends, I can continue to be independent. I can still be my own person. One can't give up, and one must keep walking on those stepping stones to renew and boost the confidence and independence.

ABOUT THE AUTHOR

Audrey Chard grew up in Port Angeles, Washington, and currently resides in Boise, Idaho. She was clinically diagnosed at age 17 with Usher syndrome type 2. Audrey received an AA degree and a Medical Assistant certificate. In the fall of 2015, she plans to start working on a Bachelor degree in Psychology at Boise State University. She loves to help people and hopes to accomplish her career goal as a Vocational Rehabilitation Counselor. Audrey likes to travel and has visited China, Japan, Mexico, Canada, and a few states of the USA.

PART 5

INSPIRING TALES:
WHO SAYS I CAN'T?

CHAPTER 23

RACING AGAINST TIME

A BANK MANAGER TACKLES THE ONSET OF DEAFNESS AND BLINDNESS BY DEFIANTLY FOUNDING A SOCIAL CLUB FOR USHER WOMEN, PRODUCING CONFERENCES FOR THE BLIND, INFLUENCING POLITICS AT THE STATE LEVEL, AND INITIATING THIS BOOK PROJECT—ALL WHILE DEALING CHEERFULLY AND POSITIVELY WITH MAJOR HEALTH ISSUES OF HER OWN. "NO" IS NOT IN HER VOCABULARY, AND SHE NEVER QUITS.

RAMONA RICE

The words "Usher syndrome" rang loudly in my ears as I sat in a chair at my ophthalmologist's office. Kneeling down on one knee, he explained the best he could what those words meant. For two hours I was stunned to the core of my being wondering how could this be happening, and then I sobbed uncontrollably.

Being hard of hearing since birth and now to have a visual field loss made me angry, very angry, because over the years I had learned to handle one disability, but two disabilities? How does one cope with a dual sensory loss?

Fear took over immediately after my diagnosis, causing me to lose my career as a bank Assistant Vice President, my husband, friends, a car, financial stability, and most importantly, my self-worth. I felt as if I had fallen into a dark, deep hole.

After several months of wasting time hiding in my home due to being fearful and indecisive, I shifted gears by creating a new life as an Usher woman. I worked with a mobility trainer who taught me how to navigate safely with my white cane, learned new assistive technology software for communication purposes, and knew I would overcome deafblindness if I put my mind to it. Believe me, it wasn't easy because it felt like I was moving at a snail's pace!

Even though today I am unable to drive, renovate homes, landscape creatively, or even do co-ed combat sports like I used to due to my narrowing visual field, having Usher syndrome has given me an opportunity to find other interests, such as going back to school for a Bachelor's degree, hanging out with my new Usher friends, enjoying my grandchildren, doing gardening, and being a very strong and passionate advocate for the deafblind community in Utah.

This endeavor includes raising awareness in businesses, nonprofit organizations/agencies, and medical/professional facilities by requesting their internal policies accommodate the blind community, deaf culture, and deafblind community under ADA (*Americans with Disabilities Act*) standard requirements. In the past six months, I have successfully had seven businesses and facilities upgrade their ADA regulations to standard or above requirements for all individuals with vision and/or hearing loss. My advocacy commitment also includes speaking at many events, writing articles and a manual, as well as doing podcast interviews and press releases to raise awareness for our deafblind community.

I was asked by a staff attorney from Disability Law Center of Salt Lake City, Utah, what the word *independence* meant to me, and I responded, "It's just a word to many people, but people with a disability who are seeking and/or maintaining their independence may say it's the most precious thing to have. It can be taken away easily if you don't fight for it. It's a given right to be a part of today's society."

USHER CHICKS IN UTAH

For several years I felt like I was the only person with Usher syndrome in Utah until I met a beautiful, smart, and lively nurse who has Usher syndrome type 2 like I do. Amazingly, I met more wonderful ladies with the same syndrome within 60 miles from where I live, which is very unusual, given that Usher syndrome is so rare. We all have a different family background, work/career path, and a different lifestyle. Because of the age difference between us, we are at different stages in our journey with our syndrome, and we are able to relate and understand the difficulties each one of us has living with it. We discuss how we can prepare for what may be ahead personally or professionally. That is when we named our group as "Usher Chicks in Utah" because we are truly Usher sisters!

We try to meet monthly for a fun activity and go to a restaurant to enjoy good food and each other's company. We prefer an outdoor dining area to avoid dim lighting and the amplified indoor noises since there are no acoustic accommodations for people with dual sensory loss, who wear hearing aids, or have cochlear implants. Disorientation also plays a big negative part for us in unfamiliar noisy places packed with people. We're always there with love, support, and patience to escort each other out into a safe zone. It shows respect among Usher sisters!

Our fun, and sometimes, challenging activities have included indoor rock climbing, indoor sky diving, river rafting, dancing, creating essential oil products, a self-defense class, and supporting charity causes. We are now thinking about a hot air balloon ride. "Pssst, I am not doing it!"

I have often noticed that when we make a reservation for an activity and request assistance in an unfamiliar facility, they have been more than accommodating. They seemed to be in awe of us and admire our spunk for living in the moment. Not only did we have fun, but so did the employees. We totally rocked at each activity event!

RACING AGAINST TIME

Why do I feel I have been racing against time? If only I had had a good family support system as a child, and if they had listened to my struggles, I know it would have prevented me from feeling so lonely and isolated. It's important to have an early age intervention to receive a proper diagnosis, adequate assistive devices, and counseling. I believe I would have known what my potential was even then.

I am still "racing against time" to make up for lost time, and at the same time, to prepare for what the future might be as a fully deafblind woman. In addition to wearing hearing aids to hear and reading glasses to read, I am learning braille, American Sign Language, and *JAWS* and *Zoom Text* (computer screen readers) to have these as a backup plan in order to communicate with people whether I have a good day or not. There is so much to do and so little time!

Honestly, I am still fearful that I will lose all my vision and hearing someday, but when that day comes I will be at peace knowing I did my best.

"Destiny is what and how you make it." —Ramona Rice

ABOUT THE AUTHOR

Ramona Rice was raised in San Diego and Redlands, California, until the age of 19, and eventually settled in Utah. She was diagnosed with hearing loss at the age of two and with *retinitis pigmentosa* at age thirty-eight. Later, at forty-two, she received a genetic diagnosis of Usher syndrome type 2A.

Ramona currently attends Weber State University in Utah to pursue a bachelor's degree in Civic Advocacy. Her goal is to continue to advocate for and assist deafblind individuals in Utah with ADA issues, as well as to help them with Utah Department of Transportation, Utah Transportation Authority, hospitals/clinics, ADA attorneys, school districts, city and police departments, and state house bills at Utah Capitol Hill. She also advocates for the support of service dogs' protection law and pedestrians' right of way Utah state laws. She is currently serving on the board of trustees with Disability Law Center. In June 2016, she hosted the Utah Council of the Blind convention in Park City, Utah.

Ramona has two successful grown children and four beautiful grandchildren. She currently lives in Utah with her second guide dog, Stormy, from The Seeing Eye, Morristown, New Jersey. This story is dedicated to her children and their families, as well as to her peers/colleagues who believed in her ability to make a difference by bringing awareness for the blind community, deaf culture, and the deaf blind community.

CHAPTER 24

HOW TO GET A MINOR IN A FOREIGN LANGUAGE WHEN YOU HAVE USHER

A YOUNG COLLEGE STUDENT GETS LOST IN GERMANY AND SURVIVES USING HIS NEW LANGUAGE SKILLS POWERED BY AN INVINCIBLE, CAN-DO ATTITUDE.

BRIAN SWITZER

The one word that I refuse to let describe me is "disabled." The word "disabled" connotes that I am not able. The word itself sends chills up my spine. I prefer the term "differently abled." I can do all the things that other people can do, but, as a wise friend once told me, I have to do it in a different way. Why is this distinction important?

When I was in middle school, a teacher told me that I would never ever learn a foreign language because I had a hearing loss and therefore, I would not be able to do it. Since then, I have made it a life mission to view anything that someone says is not possible for me to do as a challenge. Life is more exciting when you view everything as a challenge to overcome. I would fly a fighter jet if the law allowed me to do it. It is for the best that the law does not allow me to fly fighter jets.

In high school, I learned Latin. I had to learn a foreign language, and my choices were Spanish, French, American Sign Language, or Latin. I decided to learn Latin. Spanish and French seemed too difficult at the time since they were spoken languages. American Sign Language seemed too easy since I had already learned sign language and went to a school for the deaf. Latin seemed just right.

In college, once again I had to learn a foreign language. This time I took it up a notch. I could have retaken Latin, but it seemed too easy since the school only offered Latin I and II. My sign language interpreter suggested that I take German. German is a spoken language, but at the same time it is easier to hear than French or Spanish. German is more guttural and easier to hear versus French, which is more nasal. Of course, that fact did not stop me from later taking French.

In my sophomore year of college, I signed up for my first German course. It was difficult. For every exam, there was a spoken dialogue portion. We worked with partners on a dialogue and had to present it in front of the professor. Can you imagine having a back-and-forth dialogue in a foreign language when you have a hearing loss? It seems impossible.

During one of our classes, a woman from the University of Heidelberg came in to talk about studying abroad there. She gave a great talk. I was wildly interested in going. Germany was a country that I had always dreamed of exploring. It is a culture that always has fascinated me. I am forever grateful that I got the opportunity to go while my vision was still fairly good.

Studying abroad in Germany was one of the highlights of my college career. I chose to study abroad for a month during the summer between my junior and senior year at Stonehill College in North Easton, Massachusetts. I would have liked to have gone for an entire semester, but I had too many credits left to complete on my economics degree. I had declared my economics degree at the end of my junior year and had to take six courses a semester to start and finish the degree.

WELCOME TO GERMANY!

Heidelberg is one of the most beautiful places on earth. Cutting through the center of Heidelberg is the Neckar River. Its sparkling waters can be seen from anywhere in Heidelberg. My apartment window hung over the river. On one of our last days there, my class held a party along the riverbank. We played soccer and chatted the afternoon away. As dusk approached, I decided to leave the party early before the rest of the class. As anyone with Usher knows, our vision rapidly disappears when night falls. I wanted to get back to my apartment safely while I could still see.

It did not go as planned. I took a different bus home since I had taken a less direct route to the party that required two busses so I could meet up with people beforehand. As it turns out, I hopped on a bus that I thought was heading to my apartment. Instead, the bus headed for the other end of the city.

Fear overtook me, as nightfall was fast approaching when I realized my mistake. I took the bus to the end of the line and waited until it started heading back to the stop where I had gotten on. Along the way back, the bus stopped at a bus terminal, and I decided to disembark and get on a bus that was heading to my apartment. This was a mistake. The problem was that I did not know what bus I needed, and the signs were impossible to read in the fading light. As soon as I realized that I could not make out the letters on the signs, I hopelessly watched my bus pull out of the terminal.

A chilling thought overcame me. The reality of getting lost in the middle of a foreign country and spending the night outdoors alone and cold unnerved me. I was wearing shorts and a T-shirt. The night would be a long one. I would have to wait out the night until the morning when my sight would return and I could figure out where I was and get back to my apartment. I would wake up sick with a cold, or worse, pneumonia.

I paced around the terminal and found two German police officers standing nearby. I could ask them for directions. Before approaching them, two thoughts ran simultaneously through my head. The first thought was about Nazi Germany. *What if these officers were like the Gestapo?* American depiction of Germany is entirely based on World War II. The second was the adage that you can always trust a police officer to help you out. Faced with the reality of spending a night outdoors, I risked it. I approached the police officers, half expecting to be pistol-whipped with their guns, to ask for which bus to board. Much to my delight, the police officers were pleasant to talk to. One of the police officers told me what bus to board and pointed to the terminal diagonally across the street.

There was one slight problem. The terminal was blocked by a fence. It was already night, and pretty soon it would be pitch-black out. I could not make out how far in each direction the fence ran. The fence and terminal were black. With Usher syndrome, you are color blind and night blind. Black is a color that hides itself in the cloak of night. I had my eyes locked on the terminal for fear of my eyes losing track of it. I could have gone around the fence to an opening, except I was pretty confident that I would lose track of the terminal and become more lost than I already was.

I chose the obvious solution and jumped it. With the two police officers watching me, I ran up to the fence and bounded over it. I looked back to see if they would arrest me for a jayjumping law that I did not know about. I made out one police officer under a streetlight, and he was looking in a different direction. I sighed with relief as I realized they were not chasing after me with guns drawn for my suspicious need to run and jump a fence to get away from them.

I sat down at the bus terminal for a good hour as darkness enveloped me and I watched the world around me disappear. The night soon became jet-black, and I still had not made it to my apartment. At long last, a bus finally pulled in. I asked the bus driver if he was heading to the stop next to my apartment, and he replied yes. I sat down as the bus rumbled towards my apartment.

Of course, I could not calm my nerves yet since there remained one more obstacle. I could not make out the Neckar River, which is ubiquitous in Heidelberg, and I could not hear the announcements of the stops. I focused all my energy on staring out of the bus windows. I did not know what to look for. I watched as we rolled past black squares that must have been buildings. I kept looking for any clue that I had made it to my apartment. At last, I saw the pedestrian crossing light that stood across the street from my apartment. The white light cut through the night like a lighthouse beckoning me home. I jumped off and looked around to make sure I was at the right stop. After all, other stops could have a pedestrian crossing sign. Under the streetlight, I made out the silhouette of the bakery at the base of my apartment building and jumped for joy. I had made it to my apartment! I walked behind the bakery to the stairs, climbed to my room, pulled the covers around me, and crashed for the night. It had been a nerve-wracking night of overcoming challenges.

LEARNING GERMAN AS A STUDENT WITH USHER

The road to getting my minor in German was a difficult one. To learn a foreign language with Usher, I used an FM system, lip-read, and had an interpreter for the rare moments the professor was speaking English. You have to build up your confidence and to train yourself to figure out what you missed based on what you *did* hear. You have to study your bleeding heart out, as the expression goes, to get everything you can right, and even then, you will get marks off for words you did not hear on your exams, and you have to be OK with that. But, even faced with the possibility of spending a night on the sidewalks in a foreign country, I did not regret studying abroad in Germany. I would not trade the experience for anything in the world. People told me that it could not be done, and I did it. You define your own limits. Of course, after you shatter the glass ceiling of what people told you that you could and could not do, pushing yourself to your limits, people will simply tell you that you are neither deaf nor blind, because, after all, deaf and blind people are disabled.

ABOUT THE AUTHOR

(Brian, far left)

Brian Switzer has Usher syndrome type 2. His parents found out he had a hearing loss at the age of 2, and he was diagnosed with Usher syndrome at the age of 4. He was genetically tested at the age of 18, which further confirmed the diagnosis.

Brian's educational history started in Massachusetts when he was the ripe age of 3, at the Boston School for the Deaf, then the Learning Center in Randolph (another school for the deaf), Easton Public Schools, followed by Stonehill College in North Easton, through which he studied abroad at the University of Heidelberg in Germany. He graduated with honors and dual degrees in economics and philosophy and a minor in German. Now he is 24 and in January 2016, will attend Suffolk University in Boston pursuing a Masters Degree in Public Policy with a focus on disabilities rights. He is a proud Eagle Scout and member of the National Federation of the Blind. As a child, he identified himself as *hard of hearing*, then *deaf*, then *deaf and visually impaired*; now he identifies as *deafblind*. His journey with Usher syndrome has been one of self-identification, figuring out where he belongs in the world. He is still on that journey.

Brian thanks his parents, brothers, interpreter, family, and friends for always cheering him on and, in his words, "throwing their support behind whatever absurd thing I am doing next."

CHAPTER 25

TETHERED IN STRIDES

AN ARTIST, PHOTOGRAPHER, COPYWRITER, AND MARATHON
RUNNER, THIS SPUNKY AUTHOR'S MOTTO IS "MY HORIZON IS
BROADER THAN MY TUNNEL VISION." SHE URGES ALL TO "WALK
IN MY SHOES."

ROSE SARKANY

In 1980, at sixteen, I was diagnosed with *retinitis pigmentosa*. I had already been diagnosed with moderate-severe hearing loss at the age of three, and the latest diagnosis meant that I was dealing with a degenerative vision and hearing disorder. It was at that point that I decided that Usher syndrome was not going to define me.

Fast forward to 2004, already retired, down to fifteen degrees of visual field and severe hearing loss. It was then that I chose to change what had become a sedentary lifestyle by learning to eat healthy and joining a new and locally formed running club in Port Alberni, British Columbia (Canada). I started out by walking until it was no longer a challenge, and I progressed to running from one telephone pole to the next, going further every day I went out to run. Soon an achievable goal became three-mile runs, and I had lost forty-seven pounds. My self-confidence increased, and I was starting to feel like a runner, an athlete. Feeling confident, I was ready, laced up, and joined the running group on a sunny Saturday morning. My first goal was to run the Royal Victoria half marathon (13.1 miles) in October 2004.

Some of my most difficult challenges were evening training runs due to night blindness and running in trails where lights and shadows made it impossible to adjust and react quickly with sure footing and balance. Running in organized races had become too difficult to navigate around people and obstacles. Bruises and injuries were becoming a regular thing. I ran into fallen trees hitting my head and causing concussions, tumbled down ravines, ran into cars, and twisted my ankles. My training was suffering, and it was stressful, to say the least. At that time I wondered how long I was going to be able to keep up with the running as my vision started to fade away. And yet, I didn't give up.

My meeting with John Stanton, the owner of the sports store Running Room, at a local grand opening of a new store was a pivotal time in my running development. When asked if I was going to join the inaugural run, I replied that because of my low vision I couldn't. John said he would guide me. It was my first experience of a guided run. I held on to his elbow and started to run towards the horizon into dusk. As we were running, I felt safe knowing someone was guiding me, keeping me safe from harm's way and the stress began to melt away. It was such a freeing experience, almost like that of a teenager getting into the car after passing the driver's license exam. My inner self was yelling FREEDOM! I realized then that nothing would stop me from achieving the goals I had set for myself. That run marked the beginning of a marathon career that would include running thirteen full marathons (26.2 miles) to date, 2015, including the Boston Marathon, numerous half marathons, shorter distance races, and two sprint triathlons.

In 2008, after a club training run, my friend Chris Morrison and I were having a casual conversation regarding a planned trip to Boston. I was looking for a running guide, and he was looking for a training partner. As it turned out, he was a trained and certified sighted guide for the sight impaired in England before coming to Canada. We then decided to run as a team: me as a visually impaired runner and he, a sighted guide.

Preparing for the Boston Marathon was an adventure, and avoiding pitfalls became our mantra. We had many memorable training days, losing ourselves in streams, entangled in our tethers around poles and trees. Eventually we developed our own running lingo and modified our tether from a strap, which cut into our hands, to my daughter's skater shoelace. To make the tether, we then tied a silicone wristband at each end of the shoelace. Finding that right tether would become an ongoing challenge. Over the years we have tried waist tethers using our waist fuel belts with lanyards clipped to each other's belt, which worked very well. Our arms swung freely and still could feel the tension as we changed directions. As my vision loss progressed and I needed more support, we had to search for other types of tethers. It wasn't until recently, during the filming of a sports commercial, that we needed a better tether, as the one I had was not visible on camera. A young man went to a sports store and came back with three colored rubber exercise stretch bands (made with hollow rubber approximately 28 inches in length and a handle at each end). The red one was the winning tether. We removed the cumbersome handles and used the end clips to make a loop on each end. It was comfortable, light, and had perfect tension.

Boston! This was our first race as a tethered team, and of all races to try something new, we chose this one. Race day was so full of excitement and energy that it was contagious. I sensed this race was going to change our lives, but we just did not know it at the time. There were so many memories of laughter, tears, and joy at this race. Some memorable parts of this race include: the port-a-potty, Wellesley College, and the finish.

As for the port-a-potty, I never thought I would have to use it so often! I blamed it on the cheesecake I ate the night before. On one of those stops I had dropped one of my gloves. I searched and searched and could not see it, until the moment I looked into the abyss of human waste. GAH! I found the glove, but I was not about to retrieve it. As I got out of the port-a-potty, I told Chris I had lost a glove, and I was going to have to run with no gloves. He immediately volunteered to find it for me. I was so embarrassed and had to say that I accidently dropped it into the toilet. Oh, the joys of blind moments!

If you have ever been to a race event, you would know how loud the crowds can be as they cheer you on to the finish. Well, we were just about a mile away nearing the Wellesley College area, and I could hear a lot of noise. I don't like loud noises, so I decided to shut off my hearing aids. I could feel the sounds coming from the students cheering to all the runners passing by. Chris' mouth was moving, and he did a little tugging to get my attention. I then realized that I had to turn on my hearing aids again so I could hear his directional cues. Oops! I should have told him that I had done that because the noise was just too much for me to tolerate wearing the hearing aids.

And lastly, the memorable finish. We were tired, our legs were heavy, and thankfully, we were closing in to the finish line. Somehow our energy had returned as we could see the finish line, and I got so excited. I told Chris, "I am going to let go and dash to the finish." We released the tether, and I used all the energy and strength I had left and sped away. Of course I could not see Chris, but he was just behind me, still making sure I was safe. Chris and I laughed, cried, and hugged each other– we were so happy that we did it, as a team. Nobody can ever say to me that I should not be doing this. I did, we did.

(Rose, far left)

After Boston, I wanted other visually impaired and blind runners to share my experience. It was at that time that I began my campaign, *Running for Change*, to add a visually impaired category to organized running events in Canada. The Royal Victoria

Marathon (now Goodlife Fitness Victoria Marathon) was the first to come on board in 2009 and the first in Canada. Shortly thereafter, the BMO Vancouver Marathon added the category, and more followed. In Vancouver, after running the Vancouver Marathon, I was surprised with the Pioneer Award. Our goal then was to motivate and encourage visually impaired (VI) persons to lace on a pair of runners and sighted runners, to support and guide us. Today there is a growing community of visually impaired runners and guides both in Canada and internationally. The Facebook group *Running Eyes: bringing VI runners and guides together* has played a big part in bringing awareness to runners and athletes alike to reach out and be our eyes. Newspapers, news media, and radio have quickened the pace to raise awareness of our campaign as well.

Today, I still run to maintain my health and fitness. Taking up running has also helped me gain the confidence and the courage to try new things. I try to do one new activity a year that scares me, as a goal, and with each goal, I learn about adapting. I share these experiences and newly learned skills of adaption through my website in the world of blogging (www.runningfor-change.weebly.com). Some of the new things I have done that I never thought I would have the courage to do include: flying a gliding plane, indoor rock climbing, traveling on my own, zip lining, kayaking, cross-country skiing, tandem cycling, fishing, and hiking. What other adventures are yet to come? Who knows, maybe parachuting, riding in a hot air balloon, or paddle boarding. For me, this is living; this is hope to keep on living. Challenge is what drives me, and it is that fire in me that encourages me to share my life experiences. I do not want to be *that person*, sitting in darkness waiting for the light that will never return. We have to create our light to find the way.

Living with Usher syndrome has taught me many things. I have learned to adapt, to challenge myself and try new things, to educate others about Usher syndrome, and to inspire others. However, I could have never done all this alone, and I would have never had a chance to flourish had my mother not refused to believe that that I should have been put in an institution as a child. Likewise, it is because of my dad that I have the passion for the outdoors and sports. Chris not only became my running guide, but the pillar of my strength, supporting me in everything I do. He taught me all things are possible. While we cannot change the fact that we have Usher syndrome, we can change the labels society has created and bring forth support of social inclusion and fight stigmas about vision and hearing loss in general and Usher syndrome in particular.

"My horizon is broader than my tunnel vision."
—Rose Kamma Sarkany

ABOUT THE AUTHOR

Rose Sarkany was diagnosed with moderate-severe hearing loss at the age of three and with *retinitis pigmentosa* at age sixteen. Rose received the genetic confirmation of Usher syndrome type 2A in 2015. She attended the School for the Deaf/Hard of Hearing in Port Alberni, British Columbia, for three years, where she learned ASL and speech, and was then mainstreamed from elementary school through high school, graduating in 1983. During her school years, she took all the art classes available and became familiar with different mediums. She later took art courses at North Island College (now Vancouver Island University) and became a certified Interior Decorator and Paint Consultant.

Rose continues to enjoy the outdoors, and when she is not running, hiking, rock climbing, swimming, skiing, kayaking, or dragon boating, she is creating art using watercolor, pencil, and photography. She has exhibited some of her works at Passionate Focus, an annual event sponsored by Second Sense in Chicago. She is also a member of Nanaimo Lions Club in British Columbia, Canada. Rose has a beautiful daughter, Emily, and resides in British Columbia, Canada, with Chris Morrison, her best friend and the love of her life.

CHAPTER 26

MY SELF-DISCOVERY OF USHER SYNDROME

ORPHANED AT BIRTH, NOW TOTALLY DEAFBLIND, THE FOUNDER
OF SEABECK, THE ANNUAL DEAFBLIND RECREATIONAL CAMP IN
SEATTLE, WASHINGTON STATE, DISCUSSES THE CHALLENGES OF
COPING WITH LIFE DIFFICULTIES IMPOSED BY THE REDUCTION
AND/OR LOSS OF FIVE ESSENTIAL VALUES.

STEPHEN EHRLICH

I n the early 1980s, alone at my home in Fremont, California, I read a copy of my medical history with curiosity and great interest. With disbelief and shock, I learned that in 1957 at the age of nine, I had been diagnosed as having *retinitis pigmentosa* (RP). Prior to reading the article, I'd learned of the eye disease at the National Institute of Health in Bethesda, Maryland, a few days after my graduation from Gallaudet University in Washington, DC, in May 1972. I was given a number of tests for research on RP. Following my discharge, I was informed that I had Usher syndrome. I accepted it at an intellectual level, but I was not fully prepared for the emotional onslaught when my vision worsened.

I learned there are three types of Usher syndrome. I was identified as a type 1, representing people who are congenitally deaf and then become blind later in adulthood. Many type 1s use American Sign Language (ASL) as their native language. I went to see a genetic specialist in San Francisco, California, who obtained my original medical report from the Jewish Child Care Association (JCCA) in New York City. I was born a deaf orphan with limited tunnel vision of 10 degrees. My birth family's history of eye disease remains unknown. I was placed with my deaf foster parents when I was 17 ½ months old, and they provided for me until my college graduation. I still recall these early stages of my life.

My parents noticed that I had trouble finding things right in front of me on the floor. They became concerned about my vision. I had an eye examination every year, and the doctors could not diagnose what was wrong with my vision. When I turned nine, the new family doctor recorded my RP without our knowledge, and he never said anything about it. I had been taken to an ophthalmologist over 50 times for a shot in my butt with the hope of improving and stabilizing my residual vision. That did not give me any benefit.

If that doctor had been willing to share the truth, it would have made a great difference in my life. My parents could have sent me to the deafblind program at the world-famous Perkins School for the Blind in Watertown, Massachusetts, where I could have enjoyed a better quality of education and competitive sports. If I had attended, I would have learned from well-trained teachers and from peers as my role models. I would have learned things like tactile communication, braille, mobility, and other important basic skills for independent living. Instead, they sent me to an oral residential school for the deaf in New York City from when I was three until I was seven.

At the time, there were three school options, enabling my parents to make the decision as to which school was the best for me. The first option was to continue attending the same residential oral school by school bus. The second option was attending a State School for the Deaf in White Plains, New York, where American Sign Language (ASL) was used. Finally, there was the option of attending a public oral school (P.S. 47) for the deaf in Manhattan.

I was transferred to the public school. My foster parents wanted me to be treated like a hearing person, learning to speak and lip read. I had tunnel vision, which resembled looking through a telescope. I had no peripheral vision, which meant I could only see a person right in front of me. I was among the few survivors going through the failing educational system at that school which heavily emphasized 80% oralism and 20% of the three basic R's (reading, writing, and arithmetic). No one was educated about Usher syndrome until the early 1980s. I was an oral failure, unable to speak or lip-read.

As I look back upon the unforgettable and frustrating incidents in my life, I vividly recall when I first became aware of my vision problem. At age six, my deaf schoolmates and I played a softball game. I was in center field with two boys at opposite sides of the field. A boy batted a ball, and it went flying high in the air. I focused only on watching the ball and could not see the right fielder running to catch it. Suddenly we bumped each other hard and fell. We missed the ball, allowing the hitter to run gleefully around the bases to score home. Afterwards, my forehead swelled, and I experienced some dizziness. I angrily blamed the right fielder for this calamity. One teacher observed without understanding my eye problem and punished me by placing me in the detention corner for an hour. I was confused and crying. I didn't know what was wrong with my vision.

During my childhood, the boys in the neighborhood, including my foster brother, didn't want to play ball with me. They knew my inability to see well. I was always the last person picked for a team. I loved sports anyway in spite of the rejection by these people.

In my teens I was invited many times to parties at my deaf friends' homes. They always had a good time with dancing and chatting in the dark. I had night blindness, since it is part of the RP condition. I politely asked the hostess to turn the light on so I could see the dancing and chatting. Unfortunately, she ignored my request, insisting that the lights stay off. I ended up all alone and isolated most of the time.

In the fall of 1972, I enrolled at the Helen Keller National Center for Deaf–Blind Youth and Adults (HKNC). This national rehabilitation center trains deafblind students to become independent and self-reliant with their disability. One time I watched two fully deafblind men with fascination. They were chatting, teasing, laughing, and enjoying themselves using tactile ASL. I said to myself, "Why don't I try it to see if I can use it successfully?" I waited patiently until they finished their chat. Because of my long-time hunger for communication, I, self-determined, introduced myself to one of these men. I gently placed my left hand on him as he started signing. To my surprise, I could follow thoroughly and understand him clearly. The world suddenly opened up to me, and I was bestowed with that magic gift from God. It was a turning point in my life. I felt joy and satisfaction that I could finally overcome some social communication obstacles. I am thankful for the wonderful gift, and I cherish it as one of the greatest blessings in my life.

The tactile mode of communication is a great benefit. It put less stress on my remaining sight. I did not have to worry any more about needing lights to chat. I could communicate in the darkness. It allowed me to enjoy the human touch of an interpreter. It gave me the opportunity to present workshops to educate the interpreters to serve deafblind individuals better. Moreover, my friends in the deaf community marveled at my new communication skill. They realized that my usage of tactile communication made me a normal, intelligent deafblind person. They respected my dignity.

I often bump into people, walls, poles, or heavy objects, getting hurt in the process. I do it with a smile on my face, not knowing the objects are there. Sometimes I spill beverages and fall on the ground not knowing an object is in my way. Things often became difficult and inconvenient for me when I cannot see outside my field of vision, compounded by my poor balance. Usher type 1s generally have poor or non-existent vestibular function, causing poor balance.

I remember a humiliating incident when blood oozed from my right eye after hitting a sharp disc-like edge of a garbage bin, causing a cut into the eye's cornea. In the emergency room, my eye was treated and my face wrapped like a mummy. My eye healed in a few weeks, but a cataract developed. I underwent surgery for it. The eye specialist who was notified of my RP thought he had been successful with removing the cataract, but he realized he had made a mistake by not lowering the amount of anesthesia. I became totally blind in that eye, leaving me only five degrees of vision in my left eye. My reduced vision made it difficult for me to adjust.

In my 30s, I noticed dramatic deterioration in my vision. Up to this point, I could read regular print and see and identify all color hues. As time went by during this period, regular print became a blurry image. To prepare for total blindness, I started learning to read braille at age 36. I continue to use braille today, using grade two braille, including contractions. I can no longer see the colors of the rainbow. I can now only see black, gray, and white. My loss of regular and color vision transformed my functioning sense of touch into my primary sense. I now use touch to enable me to "see and feel" everything. The sense of touch is the most active, powerful, and versatile of my senses. The four other senses of sight, smell, hearing, and taste, are more passive by comparison.

DEALING WITH MAJOR LIFE CHALLENGES

Prior to my total blindness, there were five major essential values that I enjoyed for most of my life. After my vision was taken away by RP, I experienced the diminishment or total loss of these values, which significantly affected my quality of life. I went through countless challenges on how to cope with life's difficulties and making small accomplishments. It is my belief that my experiences are applicable to those who are struggling with the deterioration of vision and possibly becoming totally blind.

LIMITED MOBILITY

Traveling independently is limited unless I am well-oriented to an environment. For instance, I can move around my house, including both the front and back yards. If I leave my house to go to a building or place for the first time, I do not know where to start navigating. I need to ask a person to guide me to the desired destination. It requires practice and time to become oriented. This limitation forces me to depend on others for guidance and transportation.

NO OR LITTLE PRIVACY

If I want to do something new on a trial-and-error basis to acquire a skill and grow with experience, I may wish for some privacy. I'm not sure if I'm alone or if somebody is watching me with concern. A fully deafblind person is enjoying some privacy when he is doing something in a quiet place, unaffected and not distracted by sight and sound. Imagine this: Suddenly a person shows up without my knowledge and observes what I am doing. If I do something wrong and I'm not finished yet, he simply intervenes and takes over for me. It frustrates me and deflates my self-esteem. He does not inform me of his presence and does not ask me if I want his help. He does not understand that I would like to keep trying on my own. It is discomforting to have a person in my space without my permission. I think he's feeling pity for my struggle and does not allow me to accomplish what I am attempting to do, as if I was a caterpillar being cut off from struggling through a cocoon to get out and fly freely.

In terms of personal tasks, a deafblind person must always ask a trusted family member or friend to read a business or personal letter, such as a monthly bank statement since they are not in braille. Unfortunately, I feel my privacy is "invaded." If the blind or deafblind person is married, the best solution possible is one's spouse, whom he can trust. In spite of this solution, deafblind people sometimes would prefer their spouses not to be involved, such as in dealing with sensitive personal issues. One disadvantage of total deafness and blindness is the deprivation of a person's privacy.

INSUFFICIENT ACCESS TO INFORMATION

A fully deafblind person has very limited access to information in his daily life. In the age of high technology, some deafblind people are blessed to keep in touch with the outside world using adaptive computers and smartphones. However, they are unable to keep pace with media through newspapers, radios, and televisions. They are unable to overhear a spoken conversation between hearing people, or witness a signing conversation between two deaf persons or a group.

I am hungry to know what is going on. I have to strive to find someone willing to help with interpreting and tactile signing, but the endeavor is not easy. For example, what if I really want to know what the appearance of a farm looks like, with a young boy in his overalls carrying a bucket of corn cobs to feed some pigs in a pen? A friend helps describe the scene the best he can, including the appearance and size of a barn near the pen. He says the barn is red and big. I am not sure about what the size of the barn is, and which color the red is. I question myself, "Which red? Light red, dark red, reddish-orange, reddish-brown, maroon, or rust?" As for the size of the barn, the friend makes an estimate of the measurement of the barn's length, width, and height. However, I would like him to expand further on the details of this facility. Is there is a weathervane on the roof in front? Is there a small tower behind the barn to store oats for horses? It is not easy for a sighted person to tell all these details as he sees them. The best way to absorb and understand the exact picture is to see for yourself.

I am anxious to know how much beauty there is. A sighted person informs me the design of Indian pottery is beautiful as he sees it. I don't understand what he means unless I place my hand to touch it. If I am given the privilege to touch this object, I instantly appreciate the aesthetic things that I feel. I am then ready to agree with him about the beauty of the object's physical features.

Sports are my passion. I used to read sports in local newspapers and magazines to get statistical details on each team. After I became blind, I lost touch with that information since these newspapers and magazines aren't in braille. I have to rely on a few friends for this purpose, but they can't always give me the full information. For example, the information I receive from one of them is: "The New York Yankees won the game by beating Kansas City Royals in the 11th inning. The score was 5 to 4." However, he did not explain how the player scored the winning run, who hit to allow who to run home, who is the losing pitcher, and so on. The information is wonderful and brief, but not sufficient for me to know what happened. Thus, I have missed a lot of sports information from not being able to read sports in daily newspapers.

Overall, the core point is that as long as I am totally blind, I'm unable to have equal access to all the Information that a sighted person does.

REDUCED SOCIAL ACCEPTANCE

A part of Helen Keller's quotations states that deafness keeps deafblind people away from people. It is true. Some with or without sign language skills are frightened to communicate and interact with me unless they are willing to accept tactile signing, which is my communication mode. They do not see what is behind that barrier. This obstacle makes me feel as if I were left out and rejected socially. I don't really belong to the blind or to most deaf groups. I cannot speak, and hearing blind people do not know sign language. Not all deaf people feel comfortable with tactile ASL. Some of them are afraid to touch, or they do not feel confident enough to communicate with me. I often feel left out if there is no one around who has a big heart and tactile interprets for me. I remember a friend once telling me that it is sad that only a few people can talk to a totally deafblind person like me. What he said to me is true, because I find it difficult to make a friend who has time to talk to me or go out with me for any enjoyable activity. I truly appreciate those few who have done this for me.

LESS INDEPENDENCE

My total blindness inevitably enslaves me by forcing me to depend on others for help and guidance. Otherwise, I would be imprisoned in a house like a bird in a cage. It has not been easy for me to trust helpers who may not always be dedicated, faithful, honest, loyal, and reliable.

Some agencies in the parts of the United States serving the deafblind people administer the Support Service Provider (SSP) programs. The most common difficulties my peers and I alike experience are finding and scheduling with a paid SSP. We have to find people who are willing to train and become SSPs. The SSP's have their own lives, so we have to work around that to find times that they are free and willing to sacrifice their free time to work with us deafblind. It is, however, nice to have SSP support doing tasks and activities, allowing us deafblind to regain some independence.

Truthfully, most of these agencies are awarded some funding allocated by their state legislature or engage in fund-raising events to keep the programs running the never-ending needs of the growing deafblind community. It has been difficult to predict how much funding is given to the agency annually, since the legislators have the power to cut or raise the fiscal budget. If budget cuts occur, the agency finds it difficult to meet the heavy demands placed on it.

I am given a fixed amount of hours for the service. For example, I am allowed ten hours a week and feel that it is not enough to fulfill what I want or need for a full life. The limitation makes me feel hard-pressed trying to get everything completed as planned. Sometimes I have to give up something that is not yet finished and make new plans. For over seventeen years in Salt Lake City, Utah, I have never had a permanent SSP. The longest I enjoyed the services of the same SSP was five years. She was in her 70s. We took part in a wide variety of activities. For example, she and I went to the recreation center for swimming, weight lifting, and walking around the track. Sensing her advanced age and her job search, I knew she might not work with me for long. I asked her to help orient me to the entrance doors, the check-in booth, men's locker room (at the entrance door only), swimming pool, weight room, and track. For a few weeks I practiced finding my way. I felt ready with confidence in myself. I asked her to wait for me when I got off the paratransit bus. She walked behind me, ensuring I was safely finding my way. At last I passed the test and felt good about my accomplishments. I no longer needed her every time I wanted to go to the center. I celebrated my personal victory!

In conclusion, the sad fact is that full deafblindness itself brings many frustrations like helplessness, isolation, and loneliness. They stem from the irrevocable losses of the five major values as stated above. We must press forward with courage, hope, patience, and strength. It is vital to secure inner peace, stay happy, and enjoy tranquility within oneself, free from distractions of the world. It is very important for me to have faith in God for His guidance. His grace enables me to overcome and rise above these things. Since I have no control over RP, which has mercilessly destroyed my sight, I painfully welcome my dual disability as one of the greatest challenges in my life. I learn from it to make progress towards the completion of my earthly destiny. In heaven I will hear and see again forever. It is one of the greatest unspeakable joys I look forward to.

ABOUT THE AUTHOR

Stephen Ehrlich was born a deaf orphan in Brooklyn, New York. He was placed and raised in a deaf foster home in Flushing, New York, at the age of 17½ months. He resides in Salt Lake City, Utah, with Jana, his wife of 17 years. As a "guinea pig" patient at the National Institute of Health in Bethesda, Maryland, he was diagnosed with Usher syndrome type 1 in 1972. He became fully blind by the age of 40. He earned his Bachelor's degree in History from Gallaudet University, in Washington, DC, in 1972 and his Master's degree in Special Education and Rehabilitation in the Area of Deafness from California State University at Northridge in 1975.

As a rehabilitation teacher at the Seattle Lighthouse for the Blind in Washington state, Stephen founded and directed Seabeck, the annual one-week recreational camp for deafblind adults in 1978. Since then, Seabeck has continued operating very successfully to this day. His name was mentioned in the "Acknowledgments" section of *Guidelines: Practical Tips for Working and Socializing with DeafBlind People* by Theresa B. Smith. He currently serves on the Advisory Council to Utah State Division of Services to the Deaf and Hard of Hearing. He is grateful for improvements in the quality of life for the deafblind community. He and his wife have three wonderful grandchildren.

Stephen hopes to write an inspirational book about his life in the near future.

CHAPTER 27

MY DEAFBLIND LIFE

THE FOUNDER OF THE DEAF BLIND COMMUNITY ACTION
NETWORK (DBCAN) IN BOSTON AND THE DEAF BLIND
ASSOCIATION OF CONNECTICUT HAS NEVER LET HER LACK OF
SIGHT OR HEARING KEEP HER DOWN. SHE COMMUNICATES
PRIMARILY VIA TACTILE SIGNING AND THE INFECTIOUS WARMTH
OF HER PERSONALITY.

ELAINE DUCHARME

I grew up in a small town in Connecticut. I am the oldest sibling in my family. I have two sisters who are both hearing and sighted, and one brother who is deafblind like myself. My brother and I were both born with Usher syndrome type 1 and Coats disease, a degenerative disease involving bleeding behind the retina.

For 14 years I attended Mystic Oral School in Mystic, Connecticut, which closed in 1980. This school was very similar to the Clarke School for the Deaf in Northampton, Massachusetts. I was very good at speech and lip-reading, and I knew some signs and gestures from the time I was five years old. I picked up some fingerspelling and a few more signs while at Mystic, but we had to hide this since the use of sign language was forbidden. As I grew up and attended several colleges, I picked up more and more sign language. It was a good thing that I learned ASL before I became blind, because I have been depending on tactile ASL since I was 32 years old, 26 years ago.

I was born deaf, but growing up, I was unaware that I had Usher syndrome. While I did have problems with my sight throughout my childhood, I did not realize that there was anything wrong, or that these problems were caused by a disease. Ever since I was young, I had experienced night blindness, tunnel vision, and had had poor balance; I also wore glasses.

Because of my poor vision, I had many challenges and frustrations growing up– at home, at school, and in other places. The other deaf kids called me names, like Horse and Clumsy, but I ignored them. I always bumped into chairs, desks, wastebaskets, and door frames, and always tripped over low steps. I stayed at the dorms at Mystic. One night there was a fire drill, and I woke up to see orange lights. I tried to find my slippers, but I had lost them and rushed downstairs with bare feet. I was the last one out and was laughed at for this. I just smiled and said nothing.

At night, I always used my memory when walking or playing outside, but I still had a difficult time getting around. Halloween was my favorite holiday because I got to go trick-or-treating, but it caused problems at night. At the time, I did not realize that I had night blindness, or that there was anything wrong with my vision. My parents did not know either.

I first learned the term "Usher syndrome" when I was about 24 years old, while at a big conference in Washington, D.C., with my family. That was in 1981, and the conference was for parents with teenagers who had Usher syndrome. Since I was no longer a teenager, I joined the parents' meeting. This was the first time that I learned what Usher syndrome meant, and it hit me that I had this disease.

In a private meeting, the deafblind man who led the conference informed me that each person with Usher could lose his hearing and sight. He explained to me that the average age of vision loss was between 13 and 80, depending on the individual. I hoped that I wouldn't become blind until I was over 80 years old. However, I was wrong. I was only 27 years old when I lost my vision completely.

I learned a lot at the conference and finally realized what I had been struggling with my entire life: Usher syndrome.

My brother Paul is eleven years younger than I and has Usher syndrome and Coats disease like I do. He also went to Mystic Oral School for a few years before transferring to the Clarke

School for the Deaf in Northampton, Massachusetts. Having Usher was a big challenge for him, too, because like me, he did not realize that he had night blindness and tunnel vision.

COPING

I think that everyone who is born with Usher syndrome has a lot of coping to do, especially as they adjust to losing their vision. This can be slow or sudden, depending on the individual. It is also challenging for doctors trying to find a cure for Usher. There has been a lot of research recently, but there is still no way to treat or prevent this disease.

Paul and I feel that we are aware of and accepting of our deaf-blindness. We have adjusted to using our canes, tactile ASL, and braille. Paul used to use *ZoomText* to enlarge the print on his computer, but recently switched to using *Jaws* with a braille display in Grade One (a *Jaws* designation). Personally, I have been using *Jaws* for years and use braille Grade Two. Many deafblind people struggle with learning braille, since English grammar makes it difficult to understand for people used to ASL grammar. It takes a lot of practice to get comfortable with it.

I was eighteen years old and a senior in high school when I first learned that I had Coats disease. This was a negative experience for me because no one knew why I had this. I had a wonderful doctor in Hartford, Connecticut, who explained to my parents and me that this was an extremely rare disease – only about three percent of people have Coats. Most deafblind individuals only have Usher syndrome; it is very rare for someone to have both Coats and Usher.

Coats is a separate disease from Usher syndrome or *retinitis pigmentosa* (RP). Coats disease involves abnormal blood vessels in the retina lining, and those abnormal blood vessels can rupture easily. When they rupture, blood leaks into the eye, causing blurred and distorted vision. Later, it can even lead to retina detachment if left untreated.

My brother Paul and I were both born with the genes for

Usher syndrome. Growing up, however, most of the early and more sudden problems with our vision were most likely caused by Coats. With Usher syndrome, loss of vision happens more slowly and gradually. Because I had both Usher and Coats, I lost my vision quickly. This is because Coats disease causes a lot of bleeding in the retinal membrane. It is possible to fix this with surgery, but I was very disappointed to learn that even having the operation might not help at all. Over time, as I learned more about my conditions and became more accustomed to life as a deafblind person, I was able to accept this and move on.

Most deafblind people prefer to stay at home in order to feel safer and less frustrated. It takes a lot of planning to go out, such as finding a ride and an SSP, or support service provider. SSPs and Providers will often cancel if they are sick, have car trouble, or just change their minds. Many deafblind people can feel isolated because of this. However, there are deafblind socials about once a month that many people enjoy.

GOING FORWARD

My favorite deafblind event was a convention held by the American Association of the Deaf Blind (AADB). When I first lost my vision, I went to the Helen Keller National Center (HKNC) for the deafblind in Sandy Point, New York, for training. At HKNC, I met someone who was from Seattle, Washington, and she encouraged me to go to the convention that was being held there. It was held in June 1984 and lasted for a week. At first, I was unsure about it, but finally I decided to go. I enjoyed the convention so much that I decided to become a member of AADB. Since 1984, I have continued to attend the AADB conventions, held annually in different states.

I became a strong leader in the deafblind community and established a non-profit organization called the Deaf Blind Association of Connecticut in 1987. This organization is still running today. I was also a board member for AADB from 1995 to 2003. In addition, I was a chair person for a big national conference that AADB held in New Britain, Connecticut. Thus, I was a very active member of AADB for many years, until it slowly began to lose members for various reasons.

I am currently the Executive Director of a program in Massachusetts called the Deaf Blind Community Access Network (DBCAN). It is a program that provides SSPs to deafblind clients who request one. The SSPs allow the deafblind clients to live independently with access to car rides, shopping, doctor appointments, reading non-braille mail, and so on. I have had to go to the Massachusetts State House for many consecutive years to fight to maintain DBCAN funding, because DBCAN is supported by the state government's budget. We have managed to keep DBCAN alive and funded throughout these years, which is no small task. Without DBCAN, deafblind people would lose a vital lifeline for independent living.

FUTURE TRENDS

My belief is that in the future, the deafblind community will experience a big difference in terms of deafblind events. This is because of new technologies and in particular, the internet. Many deafblind people enjoy using the computer and internet because it makes it easy to keep in touch. It is much easier to use the computer for work and socializing than to go out and meet in the community.

I can see that technology has made a huge difference in the past thirty years. There has been a lack of events, but, in my opinion, deafblind people should make their own decisions about what to do for events and socials. Deafblind people should have their own individual goals, and personally decide how much they want to rely on each other and on sighted people.

ABOUT THE AUTHOR

Elaine A. Ducharme currently lives in Waltham, Massachusetts. She has been deaf and fully blind since 1983 due to Usher syndrome type 1. She originally grew up in Connecticut and graduated with a Master's Degree in Administrative Human Services.

She established an ongoing non-profit program in Connecticut called "Deaf Blind Association of Connecticut" in 1987 to provide support to the deafblind community there with support personnel and social opportunities. She is a longstanding member of the American Association for the Deaf Blind (AADB). She is currently working as the Director of the Deaf Blind Community Access Network (DBCAN) in Boston, which provides support personnel for deafblind clients in Massachusetts. She has been the Director of DBCAN since 2001.

She enjoys mentoring and supporting deafblind people and advocating for the deafblind community. It is her hope that deafblind people will continue to improve their quality of life and gain more social opportunities.

ACKNOWLEDGMENTS

Walk in My Shoes is the collaborative effort of twenty-eight writers affected by Usher syndrome, the most common genetic cause of combined deafness and blindness. It is incurable. This book represents how these people in a different walk of life come together with similar experiences to accept Usher syndrome, but not be defined by it.

Many thanks to Ramona Rice who conceived the idea of this book, served as its project manager, and participated as one of its authors; and to the book's executive committee: Charlotte DeWitt, executive editor; Karen Duke, project administrator; and Randy DeWitt, editor, for their contributions both creatively and factually in creating this book. As contributing authors, they have always been there for the long discussions that helped to sort out the technical details of this project and for carefully reading and commenting on countless revisions of this manuscript.

Rose Sarkany and Marisa Herrera Postlewate, PhD, were always there to question thoughts objectively and express ideas. Their patience and support contributed greatly to the completion of this book, and their personal stories of living with Usher syndrome are inspirational. A very talented and creative artist and copywriter, Rose Sarkany designed the cover of *Walk in My Shoes* and conceived the book's main title, as well as its front page introduction. Marisa Herrera Postlewate is a gifted editor and author, and her factual knowledge about the many facets of Usher syndrome is well-presented in the Appendix she wrote about Usher syndrome. She was a valuable part of the editing team.

Thanks also to Mary Dignan, a brilliant lawyer and award-winning artist, for chairing the book's marketing committee with her assistant, Roberta Giordano, and to Stephen Ehrlich, an active Usher advocate, for an exceptional job creating a comprehensive database of contacts in deaf culture and deafblind communities nationwide. Their wealth of knowledge, resources, and contacts has been essential to a successful marketing and public relations campaign. As contributing writers, their personal stories resonate and give hope to all who refuse to be defined by the limitations of Usher syndrome.

Sincere appreciation also goes to Attorney David Alexander for his help on the legal aspects of this book. As the father of author/psychotherapist Rebecca Alexander who herself has Usher syndrome, he has an insight that comes from an intimate knowledge of the disease and of publishing.

And finally, many thanks to the twenty-eight contributing authors whose willingness to share their personal experiences with Usher syndrome is what makes *Walk in My Shoes* a touching, heartfelt memoir of their journeys adapting to diminishing hearing and sight. Their determination to show that it *is* possible to lead positive, meaningful lives with Usher syndrome is what gives this book its soul.

In the spirit of the film *Pay it Forward*, these authors want to give back, to help others the way that they themselves have been helped by the kindness and generosity of others.

To this end, proceeds from the sale of *Walk in My Shoes* will be donated to the Usher Syndrome Coalition for scholarships to its annual conferences. These conferences are both a lifeline and a gateway to the future for those affected by Usher syndrome.

Alone we can do so little; together we can do so much.
—Helen Keller

APPENDIX A: AN OVERVIEW OF USHER SYNDROME

Usher syndrome is named after Charles Usher, a British ophthalmologist who first described the disorder in 1914. Usher syndrome is an autosomal recessive genetic condition that involves sensorineural hearing loss and *retinitis pigmentosa* (RP). It is considered a rare disorder affecting 6 out of every 100,000 babies born in developed countries like the United States. Routine newborn hearing screening tests are conducted now which allow for earlier detection of hearing loss, but there is no newborn eye screening for a clinical diagnosis of *retinitis pigmentosa*, which may result in a later diagnosis of Usher syndrome.

WHAT THE NUMBERS SAY

Usher syndrome is an *autosomal recessive genetic disorder*, which means that both parents must be carriers of a mutation in the same Usher syndrome gene in order for the child to have it. When both parents carry a mutation, there is a 25% chance with each pregnancy of producing a child with Usher syndrome, a 50% chance of producing a carrier, and a 25% chance of producing a non-carrier. The children of a person with Usher syndrome will be automatic carriers *and their children will have a 50% chance of being a carrier.*

TYPES OF USHER SYNDROME

There are three major types of Usher syndrome, and each type differs in the severity and the age when signs and symptoms appear. To date, twelve Usher genes have been identified, further dividing each type into subtypes, and each gene is assigned a letter of the alphabet. Although the description below is the common classification of Usher syndrome, onset, severity, and progression of hearing and vision loss can vary between individuals within each category.

- There are six subtypes to Usher syndrome type 1: (1B, 1C, 1D, 1F, 1G, 1J).

- There are four subtypes to Usher syndrome type 2: (2A, 2B, 2C, 2D).

- Usher type 2A is the most common and accounts for up to 80% of those affected by Usher type 2.

- There are two subtypes to Usher type 3: (3A, 3B).

Usher syndrome type 1 is characterized by **profound hearing loss** at birth. Night blindness and progressive visual field loss caused by *retinitis pigmentosa* become apparent in childhood/ early adolescence. Those affected by Usher type 1 have balance problems which result in much later developmental milestones, such as holding the head up, sitting, and walking. Clinically significant is that walking does not start until around 3 years of age. Today cochlear implants have improved oral communication in many Usher type 1 children. Many others, especially those of the pre-cochlear implant decade, use some type of manual communication either through American Sign Language or tactile sign language.

Usher syndrome type 2 is the most prominent type of Usher syndrome. It is characterized by mild to severe hearing loss from birth, and progressive night blindness and visual field loss that can begin during the teens or later. Affected persons do not have balance problems. With the use of hearing aids or cochlear implants, most people with Usher type 2 can hear and speak.

Usher syndrome type 3 is characterized by normal hearing and vision at birth, with progressive hearing loss, night blindness, and visual field loss.

Hearing loss usually begins during late childhood or adolescence, after the development of speech, and progresses over time. By middle age, most affected individuals are profoundly deaf. Vision loss caused by *retinitis pigmentosa* also develops in late childhood or adolescence. People with Usher syndrome type 3 may also experience difficulties with balance due to inner ear problems. They are able to speak because their hearing loss occurs post-lingual when oral communication has already been established.

APPENDIX B: RESOURCES

INTERNATIONAL ORGANIZATIONS

Perkins International
175 North Beacon Street
Waltham, MA 02472 USA
(V): +1(617) 924-3434
Email: info@perkins.org
http://www.perkins.org/international#

Usher Syndrome Coalition
2 Mill & Main Place, Suite 418
Maynard, MA 01754 USA
(V):+1(978) 637-2625
(VP): +1(631) 533-9621
http://www.Usher-syndrome.org/
https://www.Usher-registry.org

The **Usher Syndrome Coalition** strives to be the most comprehensive resource for the Usher syndrome community, bridging the gap between researchers and families.

The **USH Trust** is the largest international Usher syndrome registry in the world. It is maintained by the Usher Syndrome Coalition. See "Registry" section below.

The Usher Syndrome Coalition sponsors the annual **Usher Syndrome Family Conference**, a one-day event that is the largest gathering of the Usher community. It provides individuals an opportunity to meet others and learn about the latest research for Usher syndrome. It usually takes place in July.

The Coalition also sponsors the **International Usher Syndrome Symposium** every four years, bringing together researchers from around the world to share the latest Usher syndrome research and clinical studies in an information-packed symposium. The USH2018 combined research symposium (July 19-20) and family conference (July 21) will be held in Mainz, Germany.

For more information, contact: ush2018@usher-syndrome.org.

NATIONAL ORGANIZATIONS: USA

Many of the organizations below have state chapters. The assistance and programs available may vary.

Helen Keller National Center for Deaf-blind Youths and Adults
HKNC National Registry of Persons Who are Deaf-Blind
(See "Registry" section below)
141 Middle Neck Road
Sands Point, NY 11050 USA
(V) +1(516) 944-8900
Email: hkncinfo@hknc.org
http://www.hknc.org/

National Center on Deaf-Blindness
Deaf-Blind Services Director: Susan Patten
742 Harrison Blvd.
Ogden, UT 84404
(V): +1(800) 990-9328 or +1(801) 360-1191
(TTY): +1(801) 629-4701
(Fax): +1(801) 629-4758
https://nationaldb.org

The Lighthouse for the Blind
(V): +1(800) 284-4422
www.lighthouse.org

National Federation for the Blind
200 East Wells Street at Jernigan Place
Baltimore, MD 21230 USA

(V): +1(410) 659-9314
(Fax): +1(410) 685-5653

****

REGISTRIES

There are three registries available to those who are deafblind
due to *retinitis pigmentosa* and/or Usher syndrome, or for other
reasons. The purpose is to have the information in one place so
that researchers can find qualified patients for clinical trials, and
those affected and their families can be better informed about
future studies and clinical trials.

USH Trust (formerly known as the International Usher Syndrome Registry)

Managed by the Usher Syndrome Coalition, this registry is confidential, simple and secure place for everyone with Usher syndrome to sign up, be connected, be informed and be involved. By
being part of the USH Trust, you will be the first to know about
clinical trials.

https://www.Usher-registry.org

**Helen Keller National Center for Deaf-blind Youths and
Adults:**
HKNC National Registry of Persons Who are Deaf-Blind
141 Middle Neck Road
Sands Point, NY 11050
(V): +1(516) 944-8900 Ext. 253
(VP): +1(516) 570-3246

Email: hkncinfo@hknc.org
Email: hkregistry@hknc.org
http://www.hknc.org/

The purpose of the HKNC National Registry of Persons Who are Deaf-Blind is to provide basic information about people with combined vision and hearing loss in the United States. This information is to be used as a census of persons who are deaf-blind, as a planning tool, and for research purposes. All identifying information is confidential.

****

MY RETINA TRACKER

Foundation Fighting Blindness
7168 Columbia Gateway Drive, Suite 100
Columbia, MD 21046, USA
(V): +1(410) 423-0578
U.S. Toll Free: +1(800) 683-5555
Email: Coordinator@MyRetinaTracker.org
https://www.myretinatracker.org

****

SUPPORT PROGRAMS

The **Foundation Fighting Blindness** (FFB) sponsors an annual national **VISIONS Conference** presenting the latest research for *retinitis pigmentosa,* Usher syndrome, and other eye disorders.

This event offers another opportunity for those affected and their families to connect with others during a three-day event packed with research, living, and support sessions. It is usually held in June.

FFB also has a **VisionWalk** in June with lots of fun outdoor activities, a picnic, and a two-mile walk to support FFB. This happens annually in each state in the USA.

www.blindness.org/

The **RP Social** was started in 1998 as a one-day picnic, and it has become an annual three-day event for people with RP or Usher and their families. The purpose is to allow attendees to meet others affected by RP (*retinitis pigmentosa*) and Usher syndrome in an informal setting, and the only organized events involve local site-seeing. It has been held in different cities around the U.S. and Canada, typically during the month of July. It attracts mostly adults from the U.S. and abroad. RP Social information can be found on Facebook.

Deafblind Community Access Network (DBCAN)
A division of **Deaf, Inc.** (Massachusetts, numerous locations)
Elaine Ducharme, DBCAN Director
Email: educharme@deafinconline.org
http://www.deafinconline.org

Deaf, Inc. is a multi-service community-based agency run by and for people who are deaf, deafblind, hard of hearing, or late deafened. It provides deaf and hard of hearing independent living, health literacy and support, community access for deafblind adults, and related services. All staff are community members proficient in various communication methods, so they can communicate directly with people to assess their needs and to work with them to set up services to meet their needs.

Main office:
215 Brighton Ave.
Allston, MA USA
(V/VP): +1(617) 505-4823
(V/TTY): +1(617) 254-4041

****

ORIENTATION AND MOBILITY: USA

Orientation and Mobility (O&M) training is usually made available by the individual states through organizations providing services for the blind and for the deafblind. Leader Dogs for the Blind in Rochester, Michigan, offers a free, one-week intensive O&M course to qualified U.S. and Canadian residents.

http://www.leaderdog.org/

****

CAREER AND LIFE SKILLS TRAINING: USA

Vocational, assistive, and rehabilitation services are available through state agencies for the blind and deafblind, as well as through the Helen Keller Center. The training available can last weeks or months depending on the need of the individual.

World Services for the Blind offers a six-month training program that also prepares the VI/blind (visually impaired/blind) client for a career with the IRS (U.S. Internal Revenue Service). This training is also appropriate for those with Usher syndrome who have some hearing.

http://www.wsblind.org/

****

GUIDE DOGS SCHOOLS: USA

*Note: not all schools accept deafblind clients. Students with 20 degrees of vision or more may be accepted depending on types of eye conditions. There is no uniform standard.

California:

Guide Dogs for the Blind, Incorporated
350 Los Ranchitos Road
San Rafael, California 94903
(V): +1(415) 499-4000
U.S. Toll-Free: +1(800) 295-4050
Email: information@guidedogs.com
www.guidedogs.com
(Open to clients from Canada, also.)

Guide Dogs of America
13445 Glenoaks Boulevard
Sylmar, California 91342
(V): +1(818) 362-5834
U.S. Toll Free: +1(800) 459-4843
Email: mail@guidedogsofamerica.org

www.guidedogsofamerica.org
(Open to clients from Canada, also.)

Guide Dogs of the Desert
60735 Dillon Road
Whitewater, California 92282
U.S. Toll Free: +1(888) 883-0022
Email: info@gddca.org
www.guidedogsofthedesert.org

Connecticut:

Fidelco Guide Dog Foundation, Inc.
103 Vision Way
Bloomfield, Connecticut 06002
(V): +1(860) 243-5200
Email: info@fidelco.org
www.fidelco.org

Florida:

Southeastern Guide Dogs, Incorporated
4210 77th Street East
Palmetto, Florida 34221
(V): +1(941) 729-5665
Email: segd@bhit.infi.net
www.guidedogs.org

Hawaii:

Eye of the Pacific Guide Dogs Foundation

747 Amana Street, Suite 407
Honolulu, Hawaii 96814
(V): +1(808) 941-1088
Email: info@gdhawaii.com
http://www.eyeofthepacific.org

Michigan:

Leader Dogs for the Blind
1039 South Rochester Road
Rochester Hills, Michigan 48307-3115
(V): +1(248) 651-9011
Email: leaderdog@leaderdog.org
www.leaderdog.org
(Open to clients from Canada, also.)

Nebraska:

Noah's Dogs of Nebraska
P.O. Box 105
Louisville, Nebraska 68037
(V): +1(920) 643-0434
Email: crisisdogs@gmail.com
noahsdogs.wordpress.com

New Jersey:

The Seeing Eye, Incorporated
10 Washington Valley Road
Post Office Box 375
Morristown, New Jersey 07963
(V): +1(973) 539-4425

Email: info@seeingeye.org
www.seeingeye.org/

New York:

Freedom Guide Dogs for the Blind
1210 Hardscrabble Road
Cassville, New York 13318
(V): +1(315) 822-5132
Email: info@freedomguidedogs.org
www.freedomguidedogs.org

Guide Dog Foundation for the Blind, Incorporated
371 East Jericho Turnpike
Smithtown, New York 11787-2976
U.S. Toll-Free: +1(800) 548-4337
Email: info@guidedog.org
www.guidedog.org

Guiding Eyes for the Blind, Incorporated
611 Granite Springs Road
Yorktown Heights, New York 10598
(V): +1(914) 245-4024
U.S. Toll Free: +1(800) 942-0149
Email: bklayman@guidingeyes.org
www.guidingeyes.org

Ohio:

Pilot Dogs, Incorporated
625 West Town Street
Columbus, Ohio 43215
(V): +1(614) 221-6367

Email: kwalker@pilotdogs.org
www.pilotdogs.org

Oregon:

Guide Dogs for the Blind, Incorporated
32901 Southeast Kelso Road
Boring, Oregon 97009
(V): +1(503) 668-2100
Email: information@guidedogs.com
www.guidedogs.com

Texas:

Guide Dogs of Texas, Incorporated
1503 Allena Drive
San Antonio, Texas 78213
(V): +1(210) 366-4081
www.guidedogsoftexas.org

Wisconsin:

Custom Canines Service Dog Academy
6610 Fieldwood Road
Madison, Wisconsin 53718
(V): +1(608) 444-9555
Email: info@customcanines.org
www.customcanines.org

OccuPaws Guide Dog Association
P.O. Box 45857

Madison, Wisconsin 53744
(V): +1(608) 772-3787
Email: info@occupaws.org
www.occupaws.org

****

BRAILLE VERSIONS OF THIS BOOK

National Press for the Blind
88 Saint Stephen Street
Boston, MA 02115-4312 USA
(V): +1 (888) 965-8965
http://www.nbp.org/

National Library Service for the Blind and Physically Handicapped
Library of Congress
Washington, DC 20542 (no postal mail service)
(V): +1(202) 707-5100
(TDD): +1(202) 707-0744
Toll-free from USA: +1(800) 424-8567
(Fax): +1(202) 707-0712
E-mail USA: nls@loc.gov
Email Overseas: nlsoverseas@loc.gov

They will produce and send braille copies at a lower cost. **BARD** (Braille and Audio Reading Download) (US citizens, domestic & overseas)

http://loc.gov/nls/bardnls/index.html

BARD is a free library service of recorded and braille books and magazines for residents of the United States and to American citizens abroad who are unable to read or use standard printed material because of visual or physical disabilities. BARD works in cooperation with a network of regional and sub-regional libraries, such as the Utah State Library for the Blind (below).

Utah: State Library for the Blind
Lisa Nelson, Program Manager
Email: lfnelson@utah.gov

- Braille copies for patrons to borrow from library
- The library will also submit the braille files of this book to the BARD site so that people can download the book if they would like their own copy.

AMERICAN COUNCIL OF THE BLIND

Access USA
242 James Street
P.O. Drawer #160
Clayton NY 13624
Toll Free: +1(800) 263-2750
Toll Free Fax: +1(800) 563-1687
Email: nfo@access-usa.com

Access Braille
1421 West 12th Street
Bloomington IN 47404
(V): +1(408) 762-4836
Email: info@accessbraille.com (link sends e-mail)

http://accessbraille.webs.com
https://www.acb.org/node/1304

Exhaustive list of US-based braille document producers:

Overseas: Also see Duxbury's World Wide Braille Producers page—which includes braille producers in foreign countries–at www.duxburysystems.com/brailleprod.asp (link is external) or

NLS Reference Directories page at www.loc.gov/nls/reference/ directories/sources.html (link is external).

Many of these providers also produce large print and other accessible formats.

****

ASSISTIVE DEVICES (USA)

iCanConnect.org lets those with hearing/vision loss know about access to telecommunications such as iphone, ipad, brailler, computer, alarm clock, etc., through the **National Deaf-blind Equipment Distribution Program.** It provides training and equipment to income-eligible people and is available in each state. Apply online.

Made in the USA
Middletown, DE
05 January 2017